The *Woman's Day* Book of

Thin Italian Cooking

The *Woman's Day* Book of

Thin Italian Cooking

by *Carol Truax*

ILLUSTRATED BY ELEANOR HERMAN

Houghton Mifflin Company Boston

1978

Library of Congress Cataloging in Publication Data

Truax, Carol.
    The Woman's day book of thin Italian cooking.
    Includes index.
    1. Cookery, Italian. 2. Low-calorie diet—
Recipes. I. Woman's day. II. Title.
III. Title: Thin Italian cooking.
TX723.T77   641.5'635   78-1495
ISBN 0-395-26313-1

Printed in the United States of America

V 10 9 8 7 6 5 4 3 2 1

Contents

Introducing Low-Calorie Italian Cooking

EATING ITALIAN FOOD and losing weight is the newest miracle to brighten the lives of dieters. Low-calorie Italian food may sound like Oliver Wendell Holmes's "Glorious Epicurean Parody," but it is really not contradictory. It can be as varied and delicious as the traditional dishes that have made Italian cooks famous — and fat! Dismiss all defeatist, preconceived ideas and take a new look at and a new approach to Italian low-calorie cooking — the result will be not only superior dieting food, but delicious eating food as well.

Italian cooking has always been considered — and quite rightly — one of the world's great cuisines. It has also been regarded as too fattening for those of us who want to lose or to maintain weight, and this is a great mistake. Of course one will gain weight by eating an enormous amount of some Italian dishes (or of almost anything else), just as one can lose weight by limiting oneself to the absurdly small portions given in many "diet" cookbooks. However, one can "eat Italian" in satisfying quantities with a clear conscience, as can be seen by a glance at the number of calories given with each recipe in this book and at the totals for the suggested luncheon and dinner menus.

How is it possible to have all this and a heavenly weight loss, too? Because a large part of the Italian *arte culinare* makes use of items that are low in calories. The herbs and spices that give Italian dishes their indigenous flavor have no calories at all, and following close upon them are mushrooms, tomatoes, truffles (if you can find and afford them), and many of Italy's favorite vegetables. Soups, meat and fish dishes, and even pastas and desserts can be kept within permissible limits by using ingenuity and finding substitutes for some of the worst offenders.

There's no need to use *artificial* substitutes, none of which appear in this book. Of course you can cut calories a great deal by using mineral oil in place of olive oil, diet fruit drinks in compotes, "sweeteners" in place of sugar, and so on, although it is advisable to consult a physician before using any of them. The substitutions here, however, consist of such things as tomatoes instead of olive oil in sauces, low-fat ricotta in place of richer cheeses, and yogurt or buttermilk in salad dressings.

There are a great many ways to cut down on fats. Be sure to buy lean meat and trim off any visible fat before cooking it. Don't fry; broil, bake, or poach instead. Cooking in broth or stock adds flavor without calories. "Defatting" soups and stews is not difficult: pour the liquid into a bowl and chill it, using your freezer if you are pressed for time. The fat will rise to the top and congeal so that you can easily remove it without losing the juices that remain below.

Fresh tomatoes should be peeled unless puréed in a blender or food processor. Or buy peeled canned tomatoes.

Perhaps the newest and easiest way to cut calories is by cutting down on the quantity of high-calorie items, and this is in keeping with Italian eating habits. For example, Italians feel that too much sauce destroys the flavor of pastas — they usually serve about a tablespoon to a generous portion — whereas our spaghetti is apt to be drenched, if not drowned, in riches. Pastas and rice, like our much-maligned potato, are blamed for what we pile on top of them, and we need not avoid these dishes, for which Italy is famous, if we exercise care in making, and restraint in serving, the sauce. Similarly, Italian salads do not swim in dressing, nor do their vegetables wallow in butter.

The better your ingredients, the less adorning they require; many Italians will walk miles to get the freshest vegetables and fruits. It is well worth shopping around to locate the best and freshest food. You cannot create a masterpiece with inferior materials, and it is especially important to keep the quality up if you want to cut the calories down.

The original recipes in this book will not be frowned on by Italian chefs; they will be applauded by American eaters. This very new and creative Italian *Culinaria* is here to stay. Everyone, but everyone, should try to profit by it. Low-calorie Italian cooking is a gastronomic revelation. *Mangiamo!*

Recipes marked with an asterisk (*) are given in this book; refer to the index for their location.

Menus

You will be astonished at how well-balanced and interesting low-calorie Italian menus can be. The ones given here are for real weight loss, not for maintaining weight. They are only suggestions that you can vary to suit your family, your friends, and yourself. It is easy to make substitutions with recipes of a similar calorie count.

Average men and women consume 2000 to 2500 calories daily, except for athletes and laborers, whose needs are much higher. A diet of 1600 calories a day should produce a loss of about a pound a week. If you wish to lose more, try to restrict yourself to 1000 to 1050 calories. In the menus that follow, dinners are up to about 500 calories and luncheons are under 350, leaving 100 to 150 for breakfast. Strict diets have always been hard to maintain while letting you keep your lust for life and eating. These new diets are exceptional!

It is a good idea to organize a week's menus in advance to insure variety. Once you try these tempting dishes, you will find Italian menu planning a pleasure.

DINNER MENUS

75	Mushrooms Stuffed with Chicken Livers
235	Broiled Fillets of Beef
60	Cauliflower with Tomato Sauce
60	Mixed Green Salad I
80	Cold Espresso Mousse
510	

50	Spinach Soup
255	Lamb Hunter's Style
65	Grilled Eggplant
160	Very Orange Ice
530	

25	Chicken Broth
300	Stuffed Pasta
60	Mixed Green Salad II
100	Coffee Ice
485	

35	Cucumber Soup
315	Veal Scallopine with Lemon
45	Simple Spinach Purée
50	Tomato Salad II
110	Lemon Ice
555	

25	Mushroom Broth
300	Vermicelli with Basil and Tomato Sauce
150	Fish Fillets in White Vermouth
48	Asparagus with Lemon
55	Coffee Jelly
578	

85	Asparagus with Butter
175	Shrimp with Scallions
55	Tomato Salad II
170	Spanish Cream
485	

40	Green Beans and Tomatoes
250	Herbed Veal Chops
80	Broccoli with Olive Oil
85	Strawberries in White Wine
455	

 30 Peppers with Anchovies
330 Pan-Fried Pork Chops
 50 Zucchini with Onions
 95 Melon Balls in Wine
─────
505

100 Pasta Bits in Broth
250 Chicken Roasted in Foil
 55 Celery with Tomatoes
 35 Romaine Salad
100 Baked Custard
─────
540

 95 Purée of Green Pea Soup
200 Sautéed Sweetbreads
 95 Tomatoes Stuffed with Mushrooms
140 Italian Custard
─────
530

315 Spaghetti with Mushrooms
150 Fish Fillets in White Vermouth
 35 Fennel Salad I
 50 Coffee Jelly
─────
550

230 Rice with Tomatoes
175 Poached Cod Fillets
 55 Green Bean Salad
 50 Grape Whip
─────
510

190 Broiled Shrimp with Whiskey
200 Venetian Calves' Liver I
 60 Mixed Green Salad II
 75 Baked Pears with Ricotta
─────
525

 15 Fish Broth
375 Veal Knuckle
 60 Mixed Green Salad I
140 Peaches with Raspberries

590

SEA FOOD DINNER:
160 Baked Oysters with Parmesan Cheese
145 Broiled Lobster with Brandy
 45 Cucumber Salad
100 Strawberry Pudding

450

LUNCHEON MENUS

200 Sweetbreads Sautéed with Marsala
 25 Grilled Tomatoes
125 Orange Salad

350

160 Mushroom Omelet
 95 Tomatoes Stuffed with Mushrooms
 55 Coffee Jelly

310

225 Chicken Livers with Tomato Sauce
 40 Raw Vegetable Salad
 75 Baked Pears with Ricotta

340

160 Fillets of Sole or Flounder in Parchment or Foil
 45 Cucumber Salad
110 Strawberry Pudding

315

 15 Beef Broth
300 Chicken Hunter's Style
 35 Romaine Salad
―――
350

 15 Fish Broth
300 Vermicelli with Basil and Tomatoes
 35 Fennel Salad I
―――
350

 40 Cream of Tomato Soup
285 Sautéed Veal Chops with Lemon
 40 Green Beans
―――
365

225 Mussels with Rice
 50 Tomato Salad II
 55 Orange Whip II
―――
330

245 Broiled Chicken
 85 Baked Zucchini
 35 Fennel Salad I
 65 Broiled Sherried Grapefruit
―――
430

160 Broiled Shrimp on a Skewer
 90 Asparagus Salad
110 Strawberries with White Wine
―――
360

145 Fish Soup
 90 Asparagus Salad
 75 Baked Pears with Ricotta
―――
310

100 Pasta Bits in Broth
120 Tuna Salad with Egg
120 Baked Apples
———
340

 15 Tomato Broth
395 Cold Veal with Tuna Sauce
 50 Pineapple Whip
———
460

 25 Mushroom Broth
180 Shrimp Salad II
140 Italian Custard
———
345

 30 Chicken Broth with Escarole
245 Kidneys with Mushrooms
 50 Tomato Salad II
———
325

Herbs and Spices

Basilico

Origano

Prezemolo

THE USE OF SPICES in Italy dates back to the Holy Roman Empire. Italians made fortunes in spices and added them to everything with a heavy hand. Now they are used discreetly. Herbs, too, must be used with caution. Small quantities can be increased; you can't take them out once you've overseasoned. Herbs and spices must not overpower; they should augment the flavor of food. Use fresh herbs when possible; they are far superior. However, frozen and dried herbs are better than none. Herbs have NO calories.

NAME	USE
Basil (*Basilico*)	Tomatoes and other vegetables; pesto and other sauces; soups, salads
Capers (*Alloro*)	Soups, stews, veal, fish
Fennel (*Finocchio*)	Stuffing for roasts; soups, salads, sauces
Garlic (*Aglio*)	Stews, fish stews, soups, salad dressing; pesto and other sauces; vegetables, especially eggplant and tomatoes; meats, especially lamb (always use with discretion)
Marjoram, Sweet (*Maggiorana*)	Poultry, eggs, fish, meat, vegetables, soups, salads
Mint (*Menta*)	Vegetables, pasta, salads, fruit desserts

Nutmeg (*Noce moscata*)	Spinach, mushrooms, shellfish, ricotta cheese, desserts
Oregano (*Origano*)	Pasta sauces; tomatoes, mushrooms, and some other vegetables; sauces for veal, lamb, pork, and shellfish
Parsley (*Prezzemolo*)	Flat parsley is more favorful than the curly varieties. Almost all soups, stews, fish, vegetables, meat, poultry, salads, and sauces
Pepper (*Pepe*)	Black is stronger than white, which has the husks removed. It is at its best when freshly ground. It is more used than all other spices and herbs put together. Almost all foods except desserts
Rosemary (*Rosmarino*)	Meat, especially lamb and pork; vegetables, sauces, and oily fish (has strong flavor)
Saffron (*Zafferono*)	Rice, fish soups, fish stews, sauces
Sage (*Salvia*)	Veal, pork, liver, poultry (use sparingly)
Tarragon (*Dragoncello*)	Salads, eggs, stews, sauces, chicken
Thyme (*Timo*)	Poultry, meat, fish, salads

Antipasto

THE WORD *antipasto* means "before the pasta." It is actually a first course: either a canapé in the living room or served at the table. *Antipasti* need not float in oil in order to tempt the appetite. A colorful platter of raw and cooked vegetables, highlighted by some tidbits such as stuffed eggs, canapé meatballs, ham with melon, tiny shrimp, and chicken liver pâté will please the eye, the taste, and the conscience of the calorie-counter. Mushrooms, which are low in calories, are high in taste and popularity.

Stuffed Eggs (Basic)

Uova Sode

6 hard-cooked eggs
½ teaspoon salt
¼ teaspoon pepper
1 teaspoon prepared mustard
2 teaspoons minced onions

½ teaspoon lemon juice
3 tablespoons low-calorie
    mayonnaise
minced parsley and/or paprika
    (garnish)

Cut the eggs in half lengthwise; remove the yolks and set the whites aside. Mash the yolks with a mixture of the remaining ingredients. Taste for seasoning.

Fill the whites with the seasoned yolks and garnish with parlsey and/or paprika. Cut the whites in half before filling if you want smaller pieces.

Serves 6. About 100 calories each.

Variations

Anchovy Eggs
Uova Sode con Acciughe

Add 8 minced anchovy fillets to Stuffed Eggs* and omit the salt.
Serves 6. About 110 calories each.

Eggs Stuffed with Peppers
Uova Sode con Peperoni

Add 2 large green peppers, chopped fine, to Stuffed Eggs*.
Serves 6. About 110 calories each.

Eggs with Ham
Uova Sode con Prosciutto

Add ½ cup ground lean ham to Stuffed Eggs*.
Serves 6. About 135 calories each.

Eggs with Bacon
Uova Sode con Pancetta

Sauté 4 strips bacon until crisp. Dry on paper toweling, crumble, and add to Stuffed Eggs*.
Serves 6. About 130 calories each.

Herbed Stuffed Eggs
Uova Sode con Erbe

Add 2 teaspoons minced parsley, ½ teaspoon tarragon or rosemary, ½ teaspoon fines herbes, and ½ teaspoon curry powder to Stuffed Eggs*.
Serves 6. About 100 calories each.

Spicy Stuffed Eggs
Uova Piccante

Add ½ teaspoon paprika, 1 teaspoon Worcestershire
sauce, 1 teaspoon vinegar, a few drops Tabasco sauce,
and 1 tablespoon minced pimientos to Stuffed Eggs*.
Serves 6. About 100 calories each.

Ham and Melon Canapés
Prosciutto con Melone

½ pound ham, cut very thin (⅛ inch or less)	1 small honeydew or cantaloupe

Cut the ham into pieces about 1½ by 3 inches. Make
melon balls or cut the flesh into 1-inch cubes. Sprinkle
with a little lemon juice, fold the ham around each piece,
and secure with a toothpick.
Serves 6. About 100 calories each.

Variations

Ham with Figs
Prosciutto con Fichi

Substitute small fresh ripe figs for the melon and proceed
as for Ham and Melon Canapes*.
Serves 6. About 125 calories each.

Ham and Pear Canapé
Prosciutto con Pere

Substitute 3 pears, peeled and cut into 12 to 15 pieces, for
the melon in Ham and Melon Canapes*. Sprinkle the

pears generously with lemon juice before wrapping so they won't darken.

Serves 6. About 110 calories each.

Canapé Meatballs

Antipasto di Polpettini

1 pound ground lean beef	1 egg, beaten with 1 teaspoon
1 tablespoon minced parsley	of broth or water
2 tablespoons minced onion	¼ cup bread crumbs
1 teaspoon salt	¼ cup catsup
¼ teaspoon pepper	½ cup beef broth

Combine the beef with the next 6 ingredients. Form into very small balls the size of a large marble, making about 30. Heat the catsup with the broth in a shallow pan. Drop in the meatballs and simmer for 15 to 20 minutes. Serve warm on toothpicks.

Serves 10. About 30 calories each.

Canapé Shrimp

Scampi

1 pound peeled shrimp	1 large clove garlic, crushed
1 cup tomato juice	½ teaspoon salt
1 teaspoon lemon juice	¼ teaspoon paprika
1 teaspoon dried or 1	a pinch sugar
tablespoon fresh dill	

Marinate the shrimp in a mixture of the remaining ingredients for 2 or 3 hours.

Preheat broiler.

Drain the shrimp, reserving the marinade. Place the shrimp in a pan, brush with the marinade, and broil for 3 minutes. Brush again, turn, brush once more, and broil for 3 minutes more. Serve on toothpicks.

Serves 8. About 50 calories each.

Mussels as a Canapé

Antipasto di Cosse

3 pounds mussels
½ cup water
1 cup dry white wine
1 medium onion, minced
2 cloves garlic, chopped fine

1 bay leaf
parsley sprigs
2 tablespoons minced parsley
2 or 3 scallions, minced

Scrub and debeard the mussels. Place in a deep pot with the water and ½ cup of the wine, the onion, garlic, bay leaf, and parsley sprigs. Cover and boil for about 3 minutes or until the mussels open. Remove and let cool.

Strain the liquid and add the remaining wine, minced parsley, and scallions. Boil to reduce to about half.

Remove the mussels from their shells and put into a low serving dish. Pour the sauce over them and serve with toothpicks. You may return each to its scrubbed half-shell.

Serves 8. About 90 calories each.

Eggplant Canapés

Melanzana alla Marinara

1 medium-large eggplant,
  peeled and cut into 1-inch
  cubes
1 teaspoon salt
¼ teaspoon pepper

1 teaspoon oregano
1 teaspoon basil
½ cup white wine vinegar
¼ cup olive oil

Boil the eggplant in water just to cover until soft but not mushy, about 7 or 8 minutes. (The pieces must keep their shape.) Drain the eggplant and reserve in a bowl. Combine the remaining ingredients and pour over the eggplant. Refrigerate for 12 to 24 hours.

Serves 6. About 90 calories each.

MUSHROOMS

Funghi (mushrooms) are rich in vitamins, very low in calories, and delicious. Fortunately, there are many ways to use them, raw as well as cooked: in antipasto, as a soup or vegetable, and as an important ingredient in numerous dishes made with meat, poultry, eggs, or fish.

Marinated Mushrooms I

Funghi in Salsa Marinati I

1 pound small fresh
  mushrooms
2 tablespoons minced
  scallions
3 tablespoons olive oil
2 tablespoons lemon juice
2 tablespoons water
salt and pepper
1 clove garlic, crushed
grated lemon peel (garnish)
minced parsley (garnish)

Wipe the mushrooms with a damp paper towel or cloth. Do not wash them. Cut off the stems and put the caps into a bowl with the scallions. Combine the oil, lemon juice, water, salt, pepper, and garlic and mix thoroughly. Pour over the mushrooms and toss gently. Sprinkle with the grated peel and parsley and let stand for several hours in the refrigerator. Remove mushrooms to a serving dish and serve with toothpicks.

Serves 8. About 40 calories each.

Marinated Mushrooms II

Funghi in Salsa Marinati II

1 pound small mushrooms
2 tablespoons olive oil
1 cup wine vinegar
2 cloves garlic, crushed
1 teaspoon thyme
2 tablespoons chopped Italian
  parsley
½ teaspoon dried or 1½
  teaspoons fresh minced
  oregano

Wipe the mushrooms and cut the stems off about ⅓ inch below the head. If the mushrooms are large, cut in half. Put the mushrooms in water to cover and simmer gently for 5 minutes; drain.

Combine the remaining ingredients and simmer for 10 minutes. Pour over the mushrooms and refrigerate for a day or two. Drain and serve with toothpicks. You can save the marinade to use again and again.

Serves 8. About 40 calories each.

Stuffed Mushrooms

Funghi Ripieni

1 pound medium to large
  mushrooms
½ cup ricotta cheese
2 tablespoons sour cream
3 tablespoons minced
  scallions

1 teaspoon salt
¼ teaspoon pepper
2 teaspoons Worcestershire
  sauce

Wipe the mushrooms and pull out the stems; chop the stems. Blend the cheese, sour cream, and chopped mushroom stems and stir in the remaining ingredients. Stuff the caps and place on a glass or other serving plate.

Serves 8. About 47 calories each.

Mushrooms Stuffed with Chicken Livers

Funghi Ripieni al Fegatini

1 pound medium to large
  mushrooms
2 tablespoons butter
2 teaspoons minced onion
1 clove garlic, crushed

½ pound chicken livers
2 tablespoons water
1 teaspoon salt
½ teaspoon pepper

Wipe the mushrooms and pull out the stems. Chop the stems and set aside. Sauté the caps briefly in butter, cap side down, and then turn once. Remove carefully, cap side up, to a baking sheet and keep warm. Save any juice that forms in the caps and let it run into the pan.

Sauté the onion and garlic gently in the same pan for 2 minutes. Chop the livers and sauté in the same pan for 2 or 3 minutes, adding the water and seasonings. Add the stems for the last minute or two of cooking. Mix thoroughly and fill the mushrooms.

Don't make them too full if they are to be eaten as a canapé. If served at the table, run them under the broiler for a minute. Serve on toast if you wish.

Serves 8. About 75 calories each, without toast.

Fennel as an Appetizer

Antipasto di Finocchi

4 fennel bulbs
1 clove garlic, crushed
2 tablespoons olive oil

½ teaspoon salt
½ teaspoon oregano or basil
  (optional)

Wash the fennel and remove any damaged outer leaves. Slice thin and put into a low serving bowl or deep plate. Combine the garlic, oil, and salt and add the herb, if you wish. Pour the mixture over the fennel and refrigerate for several hours.

Serves 8. About 35 calories each.

Stuffed Cherry Tomatoes

Pomidorini Ripieni

1 box cherry tomatoes
1 can (7 ounces) tuna packed
  in water
2 scallions, minced

½ teaspoon basil
2 tablespoons low-calorie
  mayonnaise

Cut off the tops of the tomatoes and scoop out the flesh and seeds with a spoon. Reserve the flesh. Stand the shells upside down and drain. Combine the remaining ingredients and add a little tomato flesh, no juice or seeds. Refill the tomatoes.

Serves 8. About 60 calories each.

Cucumber Hors d'Oeuvres

Antipasto di Cetrioli

4 large cucumbers	1 tablespoon vinegar
3 hard-cooked eggs	1 teaspoon lemon juice
1 medium onion, minced	1 teaspoon sugar
1 small clove garlic, crushed	½ teaspoon pepper
4 fillets of anchovy, chopped with oil	2 tablespoons minced parsley (garnish)

Cut the cucumbers in half lengthwise and scoop out the seeds, leaving the boat-shaped shells. Mince about 2 tablespoons of the cucumber flesh and reserve.

Sieve the eggs and combine them with the remaining ingredients, using half the parsley and some of the oil from the anchovies. Add a little minced cucumber flesh and mix well. Taste for seasoning.

Fill the cucumbers. Sprinkle with the parsley and chill.

Serves 8. About 50 calories each.

Chicken Liver and Anchovy Canapés

Crostini di Fegatini Acciughe

½ pound chicken livers	3 anchovy fillets
2 tablespoons butter	8 thin slices toast
2 tablespoons chicken broth	

Cut the livers into 2 or 3 pieces and sauté very slowly in butter. Do not let them brown. After 2 minutes add the broth and anchovies and cook a minute or 2 more. Purée in a blender or food processor and serve on thin dry toast.

Canapés for 8. About 100 calories each.

Chicken Liver Pâté I

Fegatini di Pollo con Uova

½ pound chicken livers
1 clove garlic, chopped
2 tablespoons butter
½ teaspoon oregano

2 tablespoons chicken broth
1 teaspoon vinegar
2 hard-cooked eggs, chopped

Sauté the livers and garlic in the butter for 3 minutes. Do not brown. Add the oregano, broth, and vinegar and simmer for 2 minutes. Purée the livers and their juice with the chopped eggs in a blender or food processor. Serve on 18 hard crackers or squares of thin toast.

Canapés for 6. About 120 calories each.

Chicken Liver Pâté II

Crostini di Fegato

½ pound chicken livers
3 tablespoons minced onion
2 tablespoons butter
1 sage leaf
½ teaspoon salt

¼ teaspoon pepper
1 tablespoon brandy
6 thin slices of toast, cut into
　squares

Chop the chicken livers and sauté with the onion in the butter very gently for 2 to 3 minutes. Turn off the heat and squash the livers with the tines of a dinner fork. Add the remaining ingredients and blend thoroughly. Serve on small pieces of thin dry toast.

Canapés for 6. About 105 calories each.

Salad of Tuna and Sweet Peppers

Insalata di Tonno ai Peperoni Arrostiti

4 large peppers, green or
  sweet red
1 can (7 ounces) tuna packed
  in oil
1 tablespoon olive oil
½ teaspoon salt

¼ teaspoon pepper
½ teaspoon oregano
2 tablespoons minced parsley
1 clove garlic, cut up
1 teaspoon lemon juice

Put the peppers on the stove right over the heat so that
the skin will get blistered and blackened. You will need
to turn them several times.

When the peppers are cool enough to handle, remove
the skin; it will come off easily under cold running water.
Remove the seeds and cut the peppers into strips about
½ inch wide. Combine the remaining ingredients, in-
cluding the oil from the tuna, and let stand for an hour.

Serves 12. About 55 calories each.

Variation

Peppers with Anchovies

Peperoni e Acciughe

Substitute 12 anchovy fillets, cut up, and their oil for the
tuna, omit the salt, and proceed as for the Salad of Tuna
and Sweet Peppers*. Let stand for several hours.

Serves 12. About 30 calories each.

Roast Sweet Peppers

Peperoni Arrosto

6 large sweet peppers, green,
  red, or yellow
2 tablespoons lemon juice or
  red wine vinegar

2 tablespoons olive oil
½ teaspoon oregano
½ teaspoon salt

Burn the peppers in a gas flame until they are blistered and black on all sides. You may place the peppers directly on the burner, turning to blacken evenly. If cooking with electricity, prick the peppers with the tip of a sharp knife, so they don't explode, and place in the oven close to the heating element. Turn to blacken on all sides.

When the peppers are cool enough to handle, about 10 minutes, pull off the outer skin, holding them under cold running water. Remove the seeds and cut the peppers into strips about ½ inch wide. Place in a bowl with the remaining ingredients and let marinate at least an hour in the refrigerator. They are better if left for several hours or overnight. Turn the pieces to coat on all sides. Drain off most of the marinade before serving.

Serves 10. About 36 calories each.

Mushroom Plate Salad

Insalata di Funghi

¾ pound mushrooms
1 celery heart, cut into thin slices lengthwise
2 large tomatoes, peeled, or 1 box cherry tomatoes

2 tablespoons Italian Dressing*
watercress or Italian parsley (garnish)

Parboil the mushrooms, drain, cool, and slice through caps and stems. Put a pile of celery in the center of a cool round platter. Spread the mushrooms around the celery. Cut the tomatoes in eighths (or the cherry tomatoes in half) and place them around the mushrooms. Sprinkle lightly with the dressing. Edge the plate with watercress or parsley.

Serves 4. About 60 calories each.

Tuna Salad

Insalata di Tonno

2 large apples
3 stalks celery
1 large head lettuce, shredded
2 cans (6½ ounces each) tuna
   packed in water

2 tablespoons lemon juice
grated rind ½ lemon
½ cup low-calorie mayonnaise

Peel and cut the apples into large dice. Scrape and cut the celery into similar-size pieces. Combine both with the lettuce in a salad bowl. Drain and flake the tuna, reserving the liquid. Add the liquid from the tuna and the lemon juice and grated rind to the mayonnaise. Pour over the salad and toss gently.

Serves 6. About 100 calories each (about 190 calories each with regular mayonnaise).

Tomatoes Stuffed with Tuna

Pomidori Ripieni di Tonno

6 medium tomatoes
salt
1 can (7 ounces) tuna packed
   in water, drained
1 to 2 tablespoons capers

½ teaspoon sugar
1 tablespoon minced parsley
6 tablespoons low-calorie
   mayonnaise
lemon juice (optional)

Cut the tops off the tomatoes and scoop out the flesh, using a teaspoon. Salt the tomato shells lightly and turn upside down to drain. Crush the tomato flesh with a fork and combine with the remaining ingredients. Season to taste. You will probably want a little lemon juice or perhaps salt, depending on the seasoning in the mayonnaise. Refill the tomato shells and chill.

Serves 6. About 95 calories each (about 175 calories each with regular mayonnaise).

Shrimp Salad I

Insalata di Scampi I

1½ pounds shrimp	½ teaspoon salt
3 tablespoons olive oil	¼ teaspoon pepper
1 tablespoon lemon juice	¼ teaspoon dill

Boil the shrimp only until they turn pink, about 2 minutes after the water comes to a boil. Let stand until cool enough to peel. Devein, if necessary. Place in a salad bowl.

Combine the remaining ingredients and toss thoroughly. While this is not very much dressing, it should be enough to coat the shrimp.

Serves 6. About 130 calories each.

Soup

THE ITALIANS DIVIDE their soups into many categories, just as we do, the terms most frequently encountered being *brodo, minestra,* and *zuppa.* The words *zuppa* and *minestra* defy translation and even exact definition. They are applied to hearty soups, sometimes a meal in themselves; *minestrone,* the best-known Italian soup, is a good example, for it contains many fresh vegetables, some oil and grated Parmesan cheese, occasionally some meat, and pasta — except in the Milanese version, which substitutes rice.

Brodo is broth, a clear soup made from chicken, beef, or vegetables. It may be served with something floating in it, such as a little light pasta or tomato flesh. It is an excellent way to get a meal off to a good start, and its variations are almost infinite because of the many possible combinations of herbs and garnishes, all with no or negligible quantities of calories.

Brodetti are made with fish, alone or in combination. *Zuppa de pesce* is a form of *brodetto* that is almost a fish stew.

In Italy, most soups are enriched with grated Parmesan cheese, but it may be served on the side so that the calorie-conscious can avoid it while the more fortunate can help themselves freely.

Beef Broth

Brodo di Manzo I

2 pounds beef (shin or shank
   or rump)
1 shank bone with marrow,
   about 2 pounds
1 carrot, scraped and chopped
1 onion, chopped
1 stalk celery, scraped and
   chopped

1 ripe tomato
2 sprigs parsley
1 bay leaf
2 teaspoons salt
½ teaspoon pepper
4 quarts water

Place all of the ingredients in a large heavy pot and cover with the water. Bring to a boil and skim. Cover, reduce heat, and simmer gently for 3 to 3½ hours. Skim off froth if necessary. Strain and chill. When cold, lift fat from the top and discard.

Yield is about 3 quarts. This broth may be used as a basis for other soups or served as broth.

Serves 12. About 25 calories each.

Quick Beef Broth

Brodo di Manzo II

1½ pounds lean round steak
1 stalk celery with leaves
1 medium onion
1 carrot

1 sprig parsley
1 tomato
1½ teaspoons salt

Place all the ingredients in a deep kettle. Cover with about 2 quarts of cold water. Bring to a boil and skim. Cover and simmer for 30 minutes, until the beef is tender. Strain.

Serves 6. About 25 calories each.

Chicken Broth

Brodo di Pollo

1 4-pound hen
6 cups water
2 stalks celery with leaves,
    coarsely chopped
1 carrot, coarsely chopped

3 sprigs parsley
4 peppercorns
1 teaspoon salt
2 or 3 plum tomatoes, fresh or
    canned (optional)

Put the hen and giblets into cold water with the remaining ingredients. Cover and simmer for 2 to 3 hours until the hen is tender. Strain, cool, and remove the fat. The chicken can be used in leftover recipes.

About 5 cups. About 25 calories each.

Chicken Broth with Escarole

Brodo di Pollo e Escarola

4 cups chicken broth
2 cups chopped escarole
1 tablespoon lemon juice

½ teaspoon grated lemon rind
¼ teaspoon pepper

Bring the broth to a boil and add the remaining ingredients. Simmer, covered, for 10 minutes. Adjust seasoning.

Serves 4. About 30 calories each.

Chicken Broth with Beaten Egg

Stracciatella

4 cups chicken broth
2 eggs

2 tablespoons grated
    Parmesan cheese

Bring the broth to a boil. Beat the eggs and stir in the cheese. Add the egg mixture to the boiling broth, stirring constantly with a whisk. Do not cook more than 1 minute. The egg should shred into a ragged mixture in the soup.

Serves 4. About 100 calories each.

Fish Broth

Brodo di Pesce

1 pound fish heads, bones, and
   trimmings
½ pound any white fish

2 teaspoons salt
¼ teaspoon white pepper
¼ teaspoon dill

Place all of the ingredients in a pot with water to cover (about 2 quarts). Cover and simmer for 1 to 1½ hours. Strain.

About 6 cups. About 15 calories each.

Tomato Broth

Brodo di Pomidoro

2 cups tomato juice
3 cups broth, chicken or beef

pinch oregano

Heat the tomato juice and broth together and add the oregano.

Serves 6. About 15 calories each.

Cold Tomato Soup

Brodo di Pomidoro Freddo

1 envelope unflavored gelatin
2 cups tomato juice
2 cups chicken broth or 2 cups
   water and 2 chicken
   bouillon cubes

pinch sugar
¼ teaspoon pepper

Soften the gelatin in a little water. Heat the tomato juice and broth together. Add the gelatin and stir until it is dissolved. Add the sugar and pepper. Serve tepid or cold.

Serves 4. About 20 calories each.

Mushroom Broth

Brodo di Funghi

3 cups chicken broth
1 cup beef broth

½ pound mushrooms, sliced
⅛ teaspoon oregano

Heat the broths together. Mince half the mushrooms in a blender or chop fine and add to the broth with the oregano. Cover and simmer 5 minutes. Add the remaining mushrooms, sliced thin, and simmer 10 minutes.

Serves 4. About 25 calories each.

Pasta Bits in Broth

Pastina in Brodo

7 cups broth, chicken or beef
1 cup very small pasta such as
  stellini, anellini, or capelli
  d'angelo

grated cheese (optional)

Bring the broth to a hard boil, add the pasta slowly, and boil until *al dente,* about 6 or 7 minutes. Pass the cheese, if you wish.

Serves 6. About 100 calories each.

Egg Soup Pavese

Zuppa Pavese

This soup is made in Italy with bread fried in butter or olive oil. It can be made with buttered toast, but in the following recipe it is made with plain toast, which is quite satisfactory if not completely authentic. Cheese is usually sprinkled over the top. We suggest passing it.

7 cups broth
6 eggs
6 pieces of toast

grated Parmesan cheese
(optional)

Heat the broth until simmering. Slip the eggs in carefully, one or two at a time, depending upon the size of the pan. Place a piece of toast in each of 6 heated bowls. With a slotted spoon, transfer an egg to each piece of toast and pour a cup of broth over all.

Another method is to put the raw egg on the toast and pour the boiling broth slowly over. This will set the white somewhat and result in a very soft egg.

A third way is to put the egg on the toast and pour the hot broth over and put the bowls in a 350° oven until the white is set.

In all cases, be very careful not to break the egg yolk. Pass the grated cheese.

Serves 6. About 170 calories each without cheese.

Egg Drop Soup

Minestra di Uova e Trippa

1 egg, slightly beaten
1 tablespoon grated
  Parmesan cheese
¼ cup skim milk

½ teaspoon salt
¼ teaspoon pepper
1 tablespoon butter
1 quart chicken broth

Combine the egg with the cheese, milk, salt, and pepper. Mix thoroughly. Cook gently in the butter until firm. Remove and set aside. When cool enough to handle, cut into strips about ¼ inch wide and 1½ inches long. Heat the broth. Divide the egg among 4 soup bowls and pour the very hot broth over.

Serves 4. About 95 calories each.

Celery Soup

Minestra di Sedano

1 large onion, chopped
1 tablespoon olive oil
1 bunch (head) celery
1 can (4 ounces) tomato
   purée or 2 ounces tomato
   paste

6 cups beef broth, boiling
¼ cup rice

Sauté the onion in the oil until it is light brown. Meanwhile, scrape the celery and cut it into small dice or purée it in the food processor for 30 seconds or less. Add the celery to the onion, stir, and add the tomato purée or paste. Slowly add the boiling broth while stirring. Cover tight and simmer for about 30 minutes.

Stir in the rice and simmer 15 minutes. Adjust seasoning.

Serves 6. About 115 calories each.

Spinach Soup

Zuppa di Spinaci

2 pounds fresh or 2 packages
   frozen spinach
1 clove garlic, minced
1 tablespoon butter

1 tablespoon oil
5 cups chicken broth
1 cup milk or skim milk
salt and pepper

Wash the spinach and cook in 1 cup water until wilted. If using frozen spinach, cook according to package directions, adding ½ cup water. Purée in a blender, reserving the cooking water.

Brown the garlic in the butter and oil. Add the spinach and stir. Transfer to a pot. Add the broth and 1 cup of liquid from the spinach and simmer for 3 minutes. Add the milk and salt and pepper to taste — the amount will depend upon the seasoning in the broth. Simmer for 2 minutes while stirring.

Serves 6. About 50 calories each.

Green Bean Soup

Minestra di Fagiolini

2 cups cooked green beans
1 cup water
1½ cups skim milk
2 tablespoons dry skim milk

½ teaspoon salt
¼ teaspoon pepper
¼ teaspoon basil

Purée the green beans and water in a blender. Transfer to a pot, add the remaining ingredients, and heat.
Serves 4. About 70 calories each.

Cucumber Soup

Minestra di Cetrioli

1 large cucumber, cut up
1 small onion, chopped
3 cups buttermilk

salt and pepper
minced chives or parsley
  (garnish)

Purée the cucumber and onion in the blender with 1 cup of the buttermilk. Transfer to a pot. Add the remaining buttermilk and salt and pepper and heat for a few minutes while stirring. Serve hot or cold garnished with the chives or parsley.
Serves 4. About 35 calories each.

Sweet Pepper and Tomato Soup

Acguacotta

2 onions, sliced thin
2 tablespoons olive oil
½ pound sweet peppers, red or
  green
2 stalks celery, cut into thin
  strips
1 pound tomatoes, peeled and
  chopped

1 teaspoon salt
¼ teaspoon pepper
7 cups water
2 eggs
3 tablespoons grated
  Parmesan cheese
8 slices toast (optional)

Sauté the onion in the oil until transparent, not brown. Seed the peppers and slice into thin strips; add to the onions with the celery. Stir for a minute; then add tomatoes, salt, and pepper and cover and simmer for half an hour. Add the water and simmer for 10 minutes.

Meanwhile, beat the eggs and stir in the cheese.

Pour the soup into heated bowls or a tureen and stir in the egg mixture. Serve at once. If using toast, place it in the individual bowls before ladling in the soup.

Serves 8. About 100 calories each; add 60 calories for the toast.

Cream of Tomato Soup

Zuppa di Crema di Pomidoro

1 cup tomato juice
2 fresh tomatoes, peeled
2 tablespoons skim milk
   powder
1½ cups water

1 cup skim milk
½ teaspoon salt
¼ teaspoon pepper
½ teaspoon sugar

Purée the tomato juice and the tomatoes in a blender. Transfer to a pot. Add the milk powder combined with the water and the remaining ingredients and heat, stirring once or twice.

Serves 4. About 40 calories each.

Purée of Green Pea Soup

Zuppa di Purè di Piselli

1½ pounds fresh or 1 package
   (10 ounces) frozen green
   peas
3 cups water
3 bouillon cubes
¼ cup minced onion

½ clove garlic, crushed
1 tablespoon olive oil
1 cup tomatoes, peeled,
   seeded, and chopped
1 teaspoon salt
¼ teaspoon pepper

Cook the peas in 2 cups of the water with the bouillon cubes until very tender. Purée in a blender. Meanwhile, sauté the onion and garlic in the oil until transparent. Add the tomatoes, salt, and pepper. Pour into a pot with the peas and the remaining water. Taste for seasoning. Reheat.

Serves 4. About 95 calories each.

MINESTRONE

In Italy, every one of the fourteen main regions — every city, every village, every restaurant, and even every family — has its own version of *minestrone,* the national soup. All have a variety of fresh vegetables and include some dried beans, olive oil, some herbs, some pasta (usually elbow macaroni or ditali, which is smaller), and grated cheese; sometimes a little meat is added, such as bacon or salt pork. This delicious thick vegetable soup meal has from 300 to 600 calories per serving! Here are some not unsatisfactory and substantially lower-calorie adaptations.

Slim-Line Vegetable Soup
Minestrone

1 onion, minced
1 clove garlic, minced
2 tablespoons olive oil
2 carrots, sliced thin
2 stalks celery, sliced thin
3 small zucchini, sliced thin
3 tablespoons chopped parsley
1 cup shredded cabbage
8 cups water

3 bouillon cubes
3 medium tomatoes, peeled
   and chopped
1 cup peas
½ cup elbow macaroni
salt
sage or basil
grated Parmesan cheese
   (optional)

Sauté the onion and garlic in the oil in a large heavy pot until they are softened but not brown. Add the carrots and celery and cook for 5 minutes, stirring several times. Add the zucchini, parsley, and cabbage and cook and stir for 10 minutes. Pour in the water and add the bouillon cubes. Cover tight and simmer for about 1 hour, stirring once or twice.

Add the tomatoes and simmer for 20 minutes, then add the peas and macaroni and cook about 15 minutes longer, until the macaroni is *al dente*. Add more water if needed. Season to taste with salt and a little sage or basil. If the soup is too thick, add a little more water — but it should be thick, not watery. Pass the cheese. Minestrone will keep for about a week in the refrigerator; it is actually better the second day.

Serves 6. About 130 calories each without cheese.

Milanese Vegetable Soup

Minestrone alla Milanese

½ cup dried white beans
2 slices (1½ ounces) bacon, chopped fine, or 1½ ounces salt pork, diced
1 large onion, minced
1 clove garlic, minced
3 tablespoons minced parsley
2 small zucchini, sliced thin
2 carrots, sliced thin
2 cups shredded cabbage
8 cups water or half water, half broth
1 cup coarsely chopped green beans

3 tomatoes, or 1 can tomatoes, (10 ounces) peeled and chopped
salt
3 leaves fresh or ½ teaspoon dried basil or ½ teaspoon sage
1 cup peas
½ cup rice
grated Parmesan cheese (optional)

Soak the white beans overnight in tepid water to cover. Sauté the bacon or pork with the onions and garlic for 5 minutes, until soft, not brown. Add the parsley, zucchini, and carrots, and stir and cook for 10 minutes. Add the cabbage and cook a few minutes before adding the water or water and broth, beans, and tomatoes. Cover and simmer for about 1 hour, until much of the liquid has been absorbed. Add salt to taste; the amount will depend upon the seasoning in the broth. Add the herb, peas, and rice. Cook for 15 to 20 minutes. If the soup is too thick, add a little more broth or water. It should be thick, not thin. Pass the cheese.

Serves 6. About 210 calories each without cheese.

Genoese Vegetable Soup

Minestrone alla Genovese

¼ cup white, red, or pea beans
2 onions, minced
2 tablespoons olive oil
1 leek, sliced, or 3 scallions, chopped
2 small potatoes, peeled and diced
2 carrots, chopped
8 cups broth or part water, part broth
1 cup cut green beans
½ pound spinach, chopped fine

¼ cup tomato purée or sauce
¼ pound spaghetti, broken into 1-inch pieces, or short macaroni
1 tablespoon Basil Sauce* or 1 tablespoon minced basil, 1 clove garlic, minced, and 2 teaspoons pine nuts, chopped
grated Parmesan cheese (optional)

Soak the beans overnight in water to cover. Sauté the onions in olive oil until softened, add the leek or scallions, and sauté a few minutes while stirring. Stir in the potatoes, carrots, and soaked drained beans and add the broth or water and broth. Cover and simmer for 30 minutes.

Add the beans, spinach, and tomato pureé or sauce and stir well. Add the pasta and cook 15 minutes, stirring several times. Add the Basil Sauce* or the mixture of basil, garlic, and pine nuts. Simmer a few minutes;

add more liquid if the soup is too thick. It should be a heavy soup, not thin. Pass the cheese.

Serves 6. About 185 calories each without cheese.

Bread Soup

Mancotto

1 pound tomatoes, peeled, or 1 can (1 pound) plum tomatoes
2 tablespoons olive oil
2 tablespoons chopped parsley
1 clove garlic, crushed
3 leaves fresh or ½ teaspoon dried basil

1 teaspoon salt
⅛ teaspoon red pepper
1 quart boiling water
6 slices toast
grated Parmesan cheese (optional)

Combine all of the ingredients except the bread and cheese in a saucepan and simmer, covered, for 30 minutes. Place the toast in a bowl or tureen and pour the boiling soup over. Pass the Parmesan cheese.

Serves 6. About 110 calories each without cheese.

Fish Soup

Zuppa de Pesce

2 pounds assorted fish, such as halibut, cod, flounder, or haddock
1 to 2 pounds fish scraps — heads, fins, tails, and the like.
½ cup tomato purée

½ cup white wine
1 large onion, chopped
1 teaspoon salt
½ teaspoon pepper
2 tablespoons chopped parsley
1 teaspoon dill weed

Cut the fish into large bite-size pieces and simmer in water to cover for 10 minutes. Remove the fish and set aside. Add the fish scraps, tomato purée, wine, onion, salt, and pepper. Cover and simmer for about 1 hour.

Strain out the vegetables. Add the fish to the liquid with the parsley and dill. Adjust seasoning and reheat.

Serves 6. About 145 calories each.

Clam Soup I

Zuppa di Vongole I

2 pounds soft- or 3 pounds
  hard-shell clams
1 cup water
¼ cup white wine
1 large clove garlic, minced or
  crushed

2 tablespoons minced parsley
1 can (1 pound) tomatoes
salt (optional)

Scrub the clams and put them into a pot with the water, wine, garlic, and parsley. Cover and boil until the clams open, 5 to 10 minutes (soft clams open faster than cherrystones). Remove the clams from the shells and set aside. Add the tomatoes to the broth and simmer.

Cut the hard portion off the clams and purée in a blender with a cup of the tomato-clam liquid. Return to the pot and reheat. Add the soft portion of the clams just before serving. Taste for salt; you may not need any.

Serves 6. About 50 calories each.

Clam Soup II

Zuppa di Vongole II

Substitute 2 cans (7 ounces each) minced clams for the soft or hard clams in Clam Soup I*. Omit the tomatoes and add 2 cups of water. Proceed as directed; putting all of the clams in the blender.

Serves 6. About 40 calories each.

Neapolitan Clam Soup

Zuppa di Vongole Napolitana

3½ pounds cherrystone clams   1 cup water
    or 2½ pounds soft clams   1 cup white wine
2 tablespoons olive oil   ½ teaspoon pepper
2 cloves garlic, crushed   3 slices toast
2 tablespoons minced parsley

Wash the clams under running water, scrub, and debeard. Put them into a large pot with all the remaining
ingredients except the toast. Cover and bring the liquid
to a boil. Boil until the clams open, about 3 minutes after
the liquid boils.

Put half a piece of dry toast in each of 6 soup plates,
distribute the clams on the toast, and pour the liquid
over.

Serves 6. About 135 calories each.

SOUP GARNISHES

These garnishes add zest and interest to the soup and
have no calories.

Lemon slices   Watercress leaves
Chopped parsley   Minced celery leaves
Diced tomato flesh   Carrots or celery shreds
Thin-sliced mushrooms   Slivered or chopped pimiento
Thin-sliced radishes   Shredded lettuce
Minced scallions   Beaten egg white
Chopped chives

PINCH OF HERBS:

basil   dill   mint   tarragon
chervil   *fines herbes*   oregano

PINCH OF SPICES:

curry	powdered ginger	paprika
chili powder	nutmeg	freshly ground pepper

A FEW DROPS OF:

Tabasco sauce   Worcestershire sauce   Angostura bitters

Pasta

IN ITALY PASTA is very frequently served as a first course; it is by no means limited to being the main dish. As an opener, smaller portions are sufficient, usually six to the pound. For the main course a pound serves only four generously. In order to keep the calorie count within bounds, restraint must be used. This is especially important in the use of sauces. In Italy sauces are never heaped on, but a small amount is added and the sauce and pasta thoroughly tossed.

You don't have to eliminate pasta on an Italian low-calorie regime, but you must balance your menus. When you start with a pasta dish, it can be followed by fish, broiled chicken, or a vegetable. Vegetables make a typical Italian course and are delightfully low in calorie count. With a pasta as the mainstay of the dinner, you might start with a clear soup and end with a salad and perhaps some fruit. You can't get more Italian than that! Use pasta in this new wise way and you will find it indispensable.

Pasta is made of flour, water, and salt; eggs and a little oil are sometimes added. The dough is rolled and then formed into an almost infinite variety of shapes. Some of these require machinery in order to be formed properly, but many can be made at home. There is no doubt that fresh pasta, *pasta fresca,* is better than dried, but unless you have the knack and the time or know an Italian pasta maker, use *pasta secca,* the dried type. The imported products cost only a little more and are well worth the difference. Either kind should be cooked in deep boiling water, about 6 quarts to the pound, with two teaspoons of salt and a little oil to prevent sticking. Be sure not to overcook; pasta must never be mushy, but firm enough to resist the teeth — *al dente*. Stir several times with a wooden fork or spoon; do not rinse.

The servings and calorie counts given are for the pasta served as a first course.

Thin Spaghetti with Cream and Parmesan Cheese

Spaghettini alla Panna e Parmigiano

1 pound spaghettini	¼ cup grated Parmesan
½ cup light cream	cheese
3 tablespoons butter	

Boil the spaghettini in 6 quarts of salted water for about 10 minutes (this is thinner than regular spaghetti and needs less cooking time). Drain. Heat the cream and butter and pour it over the very hot spaghettini. Add the cheese and toss thoroughly.

Serves 8. About 315 calories each.

Spaghetti with Roman Tomato Sauce

Spaghetti in Salsa al Pomidoro Romano

1½ pounds ripe tomatoes or canned Italian plum tomatoes	½ teaspoon salt
	¼ teaspoon pepper
	⅛ teaspoon sugar
2 slices bacon or ½ ounce salt pork	1 pound regular or thin spaghetti
1 onion, chopped fine	grated cheese

Peel, cut up, and purée the tomatoes in a blender, a food processor, or run them through a food mill. Sauté the bacon or salt pork. Remove, saving the drippings, crumble, and set aside. Sauté the onion, until transparent, in the bacon drippings. Add the tomatoes, salt, pepper, and sugar and simmer for 10 minutes. Cook the spaghetti *al dente*. Drain, pour the sauce over, and toss with the bacon and grated cheese.

Serves 6. About 365 calories each.

Spaghetti with Zucchini Sauce

Spaghetti alla Salsa di Zucchini

1 pound spaghetti	½ teaspoon pepper
1 pound zucchini	2 tablespoons butter or oil or a
½ teaspoon salt	combination of both

Cook the spaghetti *al dente*.

Meanwhile, slice the unpeeled zucchini into very thin rounds, sprinkle with salt and pepper, and brown in butter or oil or a combination of the two for 2 minutes, until brown. Drain the spaghetti and toss with the zucchini.

Serves 6. About 310 calories each.

Thin Spaghetti with Mushrooms

Spaghettini al Funghi

1 pound spaghettini	½ teaspoon salt
1 pound mushrooms, sliced	¼ teaspoon pepper
1 clove garlic, crushed	¼ teaspoon oregano
1 tablespoon butter	1 tablespoon minced parsley

Cook the spaghettini *al dente*. Meanwhile, sauté the mushrooms and garlic in the butter for 2 minutes. Add the salt, pepper, oregano, and parsley and cook for 1 minute. Cover and let stand for a few minutes, so the mushrooms give their juice. Drain the spaghettini. Toss with the mushrooms, saving a few to put on top.

Serves 6. About 315 calories each.

Thin Spaghetti with White Wine and Mussel Sauce

Spaghettini alle Cozze in Vino Bianco

4 pounds mussels
1 cup white wine
2 cloves garlic, minced
3 tablespoons minced parsley
¼ cup olive oil

salt to taste
1¼ pounds thin spaghetti
    (spaghettini, linguini, or
    vermicelli)

Scrub the mussels with a stiff brush and put into a deep kettle with the wine, garlic, and 1 tablespoon of the parsley. Cover and steam until the mussels open, about 5 minutes. When cool enough to handle, remove the mussels from their shells and chop coarsely. If there are some small ones, leave them whole. Strain the mussel liquid through a fine mesh or cheesecloth; heat 1½ cups of the liquid with the oil.

Meanwhile, cook the pasta in 6 quarts of salted water for 8 to 12 minutes, depending upon the thickness. Test after about 8 minutes. Do not overcook. Drain onto a deep hot platter, spread the warm mussels over, and pour the very hot sauce over all. Sprinkle with remaining parsley.

Serves 8. About 325 calories each.

Linguini with White Clam Sauce

Linguini alle Vongole

18 little neck or soft clams or 2
    cans (7½ ounces each)
    minced clams
2 cloves garlic, minced
1 tablespoon olive oil

1 tablespoon butter
3 tablespoons minced parsley
1 teaspoon oregano
1 pound linguini

If using fresh clams, wash them thoroughly and steam in a pot with ¼ cup water until they open. Remove the clams and reserve the liquid. When cool enough to handle, remove the clams from their shells and chop coarsely. If using canned clams, be sure to reserve the liquid.

Sauté the garlic in oil and butter until lightly colored; add the parsley and oregano and the liquid from the clams. Be careful not to pour in any sand that might be in the bottom of the pot. Cover and simmer for 5 minutes. Add the clams.

Meanwhile, cook the linguini in lots of water for 5 minutes only. Drain and add to the clam-garlic mixture. Cook very gently and toss and stir several times, for 3 or 4 minutes.

Serves 6. About 350 calories each.

Vermicelli with Red Clam Sauce

Vermicelli con Sugo di Vongole

2 cloves garlic, minced
2 tablespoons olive oil
1 pound fresh or canned
  peeled tomatoes, chopped
2 cans (7 ounces each) minced
  clams

¼ teaspoon salt
2 tablespoons minced parsley
1 pound vermicelli

Brown the garlic lightly in the oil. Add the tomatoes and cover and simmer for 15 minutes, stirring several times. Add the clams and their juice and the salt and parsley; simmer, uncovered, for 10 minutes. Adjust the seasoning.

Meanwhile, cook the vermicelli *al dente*. This will not take long since it is so thin. Drain and serve covered with the very hot sauce.

Serves 6. About 350 calories each.

Vermicelli with Ricotta Cheese Sauce

Vermicelli con Salsa di Ricotta

1 pound vermicelli
1 pound ricotta, low-fat if
  possible

1 cup boiling water or broth
1 teaspoon salt
½ teaspoon pepper

Boil the vermicelli in a large pot of deep water.

Meanwhile, soften the ricotta with the water or broth. Stir in the salt and pepper; continue to stir until smooth and creamy. Drain the vermicelli and mix thoroughly with the cheese.

Serves 6. About 320 calories each.

Vermicelli with Tomato and Fresh Basil Sauce

Vermicelli con Salsa di Pomidoro e Basilico

1 large bunch of basil leaves,
  about 2 cups when chopped
1 can (1 pound) peeled Italian
  tomatoes
3 cloves garlic, minced

½ teaspoon salt
¼ teaspoon pepper
⅛ teaspoon sugar
1 pound vermicelli

Chop the basil leaves or put them very briefly in a blender or food processor. You want the basil chopped fine, not puréed. Drain the tomatoes and chop them. Put them into a pot with the garlic, salt, pepper, and sugar and simmer for 10 minutes.

Meanwhile, cook the vermicelli in 6 quarts of boiling salted water for about 8 minutes. This is very thin and cooks very fast; test so as not to overcook. Drain and pour the hot sauce over. Toss.

Serves 6. About 300 calories each.

Linguini in Fresh Tomato Sauce

Linguini alla Carrettiera

1 pound linguini
1½ pounds fresh tomatoes
2 tablespoons grated onion or
  1 clove garlic, minced
2 tablespoons minced parsley

3 tablespoons chopped basil
  leaves
1 teaspoon salt
½ teaspoon pepper

Cook the linguini *al dente*, about 8 minutes.

Meanwhile, combine the remaining ingredients and purée in a blender or food processor. Heat for 2 or 3 minutes. Drain the pasta and toss with the sauce.

Serves 6. About 315 calories each.

Fettucine with Fish

Fettucce e Pesce

1 to 2 pounds fish scraps,
  heads, and the like
2 quarts water
1 carrot, chopped
1 onion, chopped
3 sprigs parsley

1 teaspoon salt
1 pound any white fish
2 cloves garlic, minced
2 tablespoons minced parsley
2 tablespoons soft butter
1 pound fettucine

Put the fish in the water with the carrot, onion, parsley sprigs, and salt. Cover and simmer for 30 minutes. Add the white fish and continue to simmer for 10 minutes. Strain, reserving the broth.

When the fish is cool enough to handle, cut it into bite-size pieces, adding any bits of fish from the bones or head.

Cook the fettucine in the fish broth *al dente*. Drain, add the fish, garlic, minced parsley, and butter and toss quickly.

Serves 6. About 350 calories each. This dish can also serve as a main course.

Pasta with Fish Sauce

Pasta alla Salsa di Pesce

2 cloves garlic, minced
2 tablespoons chopped onion
2 tablespoons oil
1 pound tomatoes, peeled and chopped
¾ pound sliced white fish: halibut, cod, flounder, or sole, cut into bite-size pieces

½ teaspoon salt
¼ teaspoon paprika
2 tablespoons minced parsley
1 pound pasta

Sauté the garlic and onion in the oil for 2 minutes while stirring. Add the tomatoes. Cover and simmer for 30 minutes. Add the fish and simmer for 10 minutes. Season with salt and paprika and add the parsley.

Meanwhile, boil the pasta *al dente*. Drain and serve in a warm bowl with the sauce poured over.

Serves 6. About 360 calories each.

Pasta with Ricotta Cheese and Spinach

Pasta con Ricotta e Spinaci

1 pound fresh or 1 package frozen spinach
½ pound ricotta cheese, preferably low-fat
2 eggs, beaten
2 tablespoons minced parsley
1 teaspoon salt
¼ teaspoon pepper
1 teaspoon oregano

½ teaspoon basil
2 teaspoons olive oil
2 medium onions, chopped
2 cloves garlic, minced
2 cups canned peeled Italian tomatoes
1 pound pasta: elbow macaroni or other small pasta

Preheat oven to 350°.

Cook the spinach in only the water that clings to the leaves, until wilted, or follow the package instructions for frozen spinach. Chop very fine or purée in a blender or food processor. Combine with the ricotta, eggs, parsley, salt, and pepper and mix well. Stir in all the remaining ingredients except the pasta. Boil the pasta for 5 minutes only. Add to the cheese mixture and toss thoroughly.

Place in an ovenproof dish and bake for 15 minutes, or heat gently on top of the stove for 10 minutes, tossing frequently.

Serves 6. About 410 calories each.

Stuffed Pasta I

Pasta Ripiena

2 large onions, chopped
2 cloves garlic, minced
¼ cup minced parsley
½ teaspoon thyme
½ teaspoon oregano
1 can (1 pound) Italian peeled
   tomatoes
1 can (8 ounces) tomato purée

½ teaspoon sugar
½ pound rigatoni or tufole
½ pound ground veal
2 tablespoons broth
2 eggs, beaten
1 teaspoon salt
¼ teaspoon pepper

Preheat oven to 350°.

Mix the onions, half the garlic, the parsley, thyme, and oregano with the tomatoes, tomato purée, and sugar. Cook the rigatoni in a quart of boiling salted water until *al dente*, about 15 minutes. Combine the veal, broth, eggs, salt, pepper, and remaining garlic. Stuff the rigatoni with this mixture.

Pour half the sauce into a baking dish, place the rigatoni on top, and cover with the remaining sauce. Bake for 30 minutes.

Serves 6. About 300 calories each.

Stuffed Pasta II

Rigatoni Imbottiti

1 cup chopped onions
2 cloves garlic, crushed
½ cup minced parsley
½ teaspoon thyme
1 can (8 ounces) tomato purée
　or sauce
1 can (1 pound) Italian plum
　tomatoes

½ pound rigatoni
¾ pound ground beef
¼ cup milk
2 eggs
½ teaspoon oregano
1 teaspoon salt
¼ teaspoon pepper

Preheat oven to 350°.

Mix the onion, garlic, parsley, and thyme with the tomato purée and tomatoes. Cook the pasta in boiling salted water until almost tender, about 12 minutes. Combine the remaining ingredients and stuff the rigatoni with this mixture. Pour half the sauce into a low baking dish or casserole. Place the rigatoni on top and pour the remaining sauce over all. Bake for 1 hour.

Serves 6. About 300 calories each.

Macaroni with Tomato Sauce

Bucatini alla Marinara

The original name for pasta was *maccaruni,* as found in records of the mid-thirteenth century.

1 large clove garlic, minced
1 tablespoon olive oil
2 cans (1 pound each) peeled
　tomatoes or 2 pounds fresh
　tomatoes

1 teaspoon salt
½ teaspoon sugar
2 tablespoons minced parsley
1¼ pounds macaroni
　(bucatini size)

Sauté the garlic in the oil for a minute and add the tomatoes. (If they are fresh, peel and chop them.) Add the salt, sugar, and parsley. Cover and simmer 15 minutes, stirring several times vigorously to break up the tomatoes.

Cook the macaroni in 5 or 6 quarts of boiling salted water for about 12 minutes. Break them into 3- to 4-inch pieces, if you wish, for ease of serving. Drain into a heated serving bowl and pour the sauce over. Toss.

Serves 6. About 375 calories.

Macaroni with Ricotta Cheese

Maccheroni con Ricotta

1¼ pounds macaroni (any shape)
1 cup ricotta cheese
½ cup milk
½ teaspoon salt

Cook the macaroni in 6 quarts of boiling salted water until *al dente*, about 12 minutes if small pieces are used, up to 15 minutes for larger.

Meanwhile, combine the cheese with the milk and salt and mix until smooth. Drain the macaroni, return to the pot, pour the sauce over, and heat for 2 to 3 minutes.

Serves 6. About 350 calories each.

Elbow Macaroni with Cauliflower

Maccheroni al Cavolfiore

1 pound elbow macaroni
2 teaspoons salt
1 medium head cauliflower
2 tablespoons melted butter
½ teaspoon pepper
minced parsley (garnish)
grated Parmesan cheese

Cook the macaroni in deep water with 1 teaspoon of the salt, *al dente*. Break the cauliflower into flowerettes and cook, covered, in a little water with the remaining salt for about 12 minutes, until it is tender but not too soft. Drain the cauliflower, toss with the drained macaroni, melted butter, and pepper, and serve at once. Garnish with parsley. Pass the cheese.

Serves 6. About 300 calories each without cheese.

Risotto

RISOTTO is featured in Northern Italy. The rice is often sautéed in butter with onion, garlic, parsley, and other herbs. The hot broth, water, and sometimes wine are added slowly, a cup or less at a time. The rice should be soft but a little firm in the center of each grain — *al dente*. By all means use Italian rice if you can get it. *Arborio* is available in America under several brand names.

Rice has about the same number of calories as pasta. In Italy, 5 ounces are usually served as one helping; here we have suggested about 3 ounces. Even with this reduction you cannot afford *risotto* as a side dish. Like pasta, it can be a first or main course. Don't have it too often, and balance the menu carefully. But do try these specially adapted *risottos* to enjoy this Italian taste sensation.

Steamed Rice

Risotto

1 medium-large onion, minced
2 tablespoons butter
1 cup rice

2½ cups chicken broth
salt and pepper

Sauté the onion in the butter until transparent. Stir in the rice and brown while stirring. Pour in 1 cup of the broth; cover and simmer 10 minutes. Add ½ more cup broth and continue to simmer. If serving without a sauce, cook 10 more minutes and add the remaining broth. Continue to simmer, covered, until the rice is tender, about 10 minutes. Taste for seasonings.

If using a sauce, add after 15 minutes of cooking and omit the salt and pepper. Cook and stir for 10 minutes more.

Serves 4. About 200 calories each.

Green Rice

Risotto Verde

1 package frozen chopped spinach	1½ cups rice
	1 teaspoon salt
1 large onion, chopped	¼ teaspoon pepper
2 tablespoons butter	¼ cup chopped parsley

Cook the spinach according to the package directions, using an extra cup of water. Drain, saving all the water. When cool, squeeze, saving all the liquid.

Sauté the onion in the butter. Add the rice, salt, pepper, and the spinach. Stir and cook until the rice is lightly browned. Add 1 cup of the spinach water and simmer, covered, for 20 minutes. As the water is absorbed, add more, a cup at a time. Add the parsley and adjust the seasonings. The *risotto* should be moist, not soupy.

Serves 6. About 250 calories each.

Milanese Rice

Risotto alla Milanese

1 medium onion, minced	3 cups chicken broth or part water, part broth
2 tablespoons butter	
2 tablespoons beef marrow, if available (optional)	¼ teaspoon saffron
	salt
1½ cups rice	¼ teaspoon pepper
1½ cups white wine or Marsala	¼ cup grated Parmesan cheese (optional)

Sauté the onion in the butter until golden. Add the marrow, if you wish, and the rice. Stir and brown the rice and add the wine; simmer for 3 or 4 minutes. Add the water or broth, about ½ cup at a time. Soften the saffron in a little hot water or broth and let stand for 10 minutes. Stir into the rice and add the salt and pepper to taste. (The amount of salt will depend upon the seasoning in the broth.) Let stand, covered, for a few minutes to steam. The whole cooking process should take about 25 minutes. Pass the cheese separately, though it is good to stir in the cheese if you can spare the extra calories.

Serves 6. About 230 calories each; about 270 calories each with cheese.

Rice with Tomatoes

Risotto ai Pomidori

1 large yellow onion, chopped fine
2 tablespoons olive oil
¾ cup rice
1 can (1 pound) peeled Italian tomatoes, chopped

½ cup broth
½ teaspoon salt
¼ teaspoon pepper
¼ teaspoon sugar

Sauté the onion in the oil until pale golden. Add the rice and stir until coated with oil. Add the remaining ingredients. Simmer, covered, for 15 minutes; uncover and cook gently for 10 minutes more.

Serves 4. About 230 calories each.

Rice with Mushrooms

Risotto ai Funghi

1 medium onion, chopped fine
2 tablespoons oil
1 clove garlic, minced
1½ cups rice

about 4 cups broth
¾ pound mushrooms, sliced thin or coarsely chopped
2 tablespoons butter

Sauté the onion in the oil until limp, not brown. Add the garlic and stir for 1 minute. Stir in the rice; when it is coated with oil, add ½ cup of boiling broth while stirring. Add the remaining broth, ½ cup at a time, as the liquid is absorbed.

Meanwhile, sauté the mushrooms gently in butter until they give up their juice, about 3 minutes. Add them with all the pan juices to the rice near the end of the rice's cooking time.

Serves 6. About 300 calories each.

Rice with Asparagus

Risotto con Asparagi

1 pound asparagus	1½ cups rice
1 teaspoon salt	about 3 cups chicken broth
1 small onion, chopped fine	3 tablespoons grated
2 tablespoons vegetable oil	Parmesan cheese

Cut off the tough ends of the asparagus and scrape the stalks up about 2 inches. Cook in a steamer, or stand the asparagus up in a pot, tied in two bunches. Put about 2 inches of water and the salt in the pot, cover tightly, and cook until tender, about 15 minutes. If the stalks are heavy it will take a little longer. Remove the asparagus to a flat dish, tilt to let the liquid drain off until it is cool, then cut into pieces about ½ inch long.

Sauté the onion in the oil until transparent. Add the rice and stir until coated with oil. Add ½ cup boiling broth and stir and cook until the liquid is absorbed. Add the remaining broth, ½ cup at a time, while stirring. After two additions stir in the asparagus and continue with the broth.

The total cooking time will be under half an hour. Taste for salt. Stir in the cheese and rake into a hot serving dish, using a fork, not a spoon.

Serves 6. About 300 calories each.

Kidney Rice

Risotto con Rognone di Vitello

3 veal kidneys
2 tablespoons olive oil
1 clove garlic, minced
1 teaspoon sage, rosemary,
    and/or oregano

2 tablespoons tomato paste
    and 2 tablespoons water, or
    4 tablespoons tomato sauce
1 recipe Steamed Rice*

Cut up the kidneys, removing the hard center core. Sauté in the oil with the garlic for 2 minutes. Stir in the herbs and the tomato paste mixed with the water or the tomato sauce. Simmer, uncovered, for 3 minutes. Stir into the Steamed Rice*, and stir and cook for about 10 minutes.

Serves 6. About 300 calories each.

Sauces

Sauces do not have to be rich and heavy to be good; actually, they should enhance or complement rather than overwhelm. Using tomatoes instead of oil is an old Italian custom, especially in the South, where tomatoes are good and cheap. They are also low in calories, as are other sauce ingredients such as broth, mushrooms, scallions, herbs, and even wine. The alcoholic calories in wine evaporate very quickly with cooking.

Basic Tomato Sauce

Salsa Semplice di Pomidoro

1 pound fresh tomatoes or 1
   can (14 ounces) peeled
   Italian tomatoes
1 clove garlic, crushed
1 tablespoon olive oil

½ teaspoon salt
¼ teaspoon pepper
¼ teaspoon sugar
½ teaspoon basil or oregano
   (optional)

If using canned tomatoes, purée in food processor or blender briefly. If using fresh, peel, seed, and chop. Sauté the garlic in the oil for a minute and add the tomatoes and seasonings. Simmer for 30 minutes, stirring frequently. The sauce should be thick and smooth. Taste for seasoning.

About 1¼ cups; sauce for 6 servings. About 35 calories each.

Fresh Tomato Sauce

Sugo di Pomidoro Fresco

1½ pounds fresh tomatoes,
   preferably plum, chopped
1 carrot, chopped
1 stalk celery, scraped and
   chopped
1 onion, chopped

2 sprigs parsley
3 leaves fresh or ½ teaspoon
   dried basil
1 teaspoon salt
½ teaspoon pepper
½ teaspoon sugar

Put the tomatoes into a saucepan with the remaining ingredients and cook uncovered for 30 minutes, stirring from time to time. Put through a food mill, food processor, or blender and return to the pot; simmer for 10 minutes more until thick.

About 1½ cups; sauce for 6 servings. About 45 calories each.

Country-Style Spaghetti Sauce

Salsa alla Rustica

2 cloves garlic, crushed
1 cup minced onion
1 tablespoon olive oil
4 anchovy fillets, chopped
2 tablespoons minced parsley

½ teaspoon dried or 1
   teaspoon minced fresh
   oregano or basil
½ cup broth

Sauté the garlic and onion in the oil until light brown. Stir in the remaining ingredients; stir and cook until the anchovies dissolve and the sauce becomes a paste.

If using fresh herbs, stir in when the sauce is cooked. If the sauce is too thick, add a tablespoon of water.

About 1¼ cups; serves 6. About 35 calories each.

Tomato Sauce with Basil

Salsa di Pomidoro al Basilico

1 tablespoon butter
½ tablespoon oil
2 tablespoons minced onion
1½ pounds tomatoes, peeled
  and cut up, fresh or canned

½ teaspoon salt
¼ teaspoon pepper
1 cup or more coarsely
  chopped fresh basil

Heat the butter and oil together and sauté the onion until light brown; add the tomatoes, salt, and pepper. Cover and simmer for 30 minutes. Stir in the basil and heat. Serve over pasta.

About 1½ cups; serves 6. About 50 calories each.

Anchovy-Tomato Sauce

Salsa di Acciughe con Pomidoro

2 cloves garlic, minced, or 1
  onion, chopped fine
1 tablespoon olive oil
1 can (2 ounces) anchovy
  fillets, chopped

2 cups, chopped, or 1 can (14
  ounces) peeled Italiam plum
  tomatoes
1 tablespoon minced parsley
salt and pepper

Sauté the garlic or onion in the olive oil and 1 tablespoon of the oil from the anchovies until lightly browned. Add the anchovies and stir for 2 to 3 minutes. Add the tomatoes and parsley and simmer for 30 minutes. Adjust seasoning to taste, you will need very little salt.

About 1½ cups; serves 6. About 65 calories each.

Mushroom and Tomato Sauce

Salsa di Funghi e Pomidoro

1 pound mushrooms, sliced
2 cloves garlic, minced
1 tablespoon oil
1 tablespoon butter
1 can (7 ounces) tomato purée

2 tablespoons water
2 tablespoons fresh or 1
  teaspoon dried basil
1 teaspoon salt
2 tablespoons minced parsley

Sauté the mushrooms and garlic in the oil and butter for 2 minutes while stirring. Add the remaining ingredients and simmer for 2 minutes more.

About 2 cups. Serves 12. About 50 calories each.

Mariner's Sauce

Salsa Marinara

1 cup chopped onions
1 clove garlic, minced
2 tablespoons olive oil
1 can (2 pounds, 3 ounces)
  Italian plum tomatoes
1 teaspoon salt

¼ teaspoon pepper
1 teaspoon sugar
1 teaspoon dried or 1
  tablespoon minced fresh
  oregano

Sauté the onions and garlic in the oil until light brown. Add the remaining ingredients; cover and simmer gently for 30 minutes. Purée in a blender or force through a sieve. Return to the pot, cover, and simmer for 15 minutes.

About 3½ cups; serves 12. About 50 calories each.

Variations

Anchovy Marinara

Add 4 chopped fillets of anchovies in the last 10 minutes of cooking.

Mushroom Marinara

Add ½ pound sliced mushrooms in the last 10 minutes of cooking.

Basil Marinara

Reduce the oregano to ¼ teaspoon dried or ¼ tablespoon fresh and add 1 teaspoon dried or 1 tablespoon fresh chopped basil.

PESTO

THE WORD *pesto* means pounded, and this delicious sauce for pasta is traditionally made by pounding fresh basil with a pestle in a mortar. However, it is easier to use a blender or food processor, but be careful not to make too smooth a purée. Turn on the blender for half a minute or less, scrape the *pesto* down, and repeat. It is usually made from quantities of fresh basil, some olive oil, garlic, Parmesan cheese, and pine nuts or walnuts. This sauce is also good in soups and on some vegetables. It can be frozen without the garlic, which should be added just before serving. Although *pesto* is not low in calories, it is so flavorful that it can be used sparingly.

Here is an Italian recipe for *pesto*. Compare it with the ones recommended in this book.

PESTO

	Calories
2 cups tightly packed basil leaves	100
½ cup pine nuts (*pignoli*)	335
½ cup grated Parmesan cheese	
(or part Romano)	445
1 cup olive oil	2000
2 teaspoons chopped garlic	0
6 servings, 480 calories each	2880

Basil Sauce I

Pesto I

2 cups chopped fresh basil
   leaves
2 tablespoons chopped
   Italian parsley
3 tablespoons olive oil
3 cloves garlic, cut up

¼ cup pine nuts (*pignoli*)
2 tablespoons grated
   Parmesan or Romano
   cheese
3 tablespoons water

If using a food processor, put all the ingredients in, half at a time, and blend for a few seconds; scrape down and blend again for only a few seconds. If using a blender, put the liquid in first, add the other ingredients, and blend for 1 minute. If chopping by hand, mince as fine as possible or use a pestle and mortar and a garlic press.

About 1 cup; for pasta for 6. About 125 calories each.

Basil Sauce II

Pesto II

3 cups tightly packed basil
   leaves
3 cloves garlic, crushed
3 tablespoons pine nuts
   (*pignoli*) and/or walnuts
3 tablespoons olive oil

1 teaspoon salt
2 tablespoons grated
   Parmesan cheese
1 tablespoon grated Pecorina
   or Romano cheese

Put all of the ingredients except the cheeses into a blender or food processor and purée until smooth. Scrape the mixture down with a rubber spatula several times. Stir in the cheese, mixing thoroughly.

To serve, stir a tablespoon of hot water into each ½ cup, and use ½ cup of sauce for 1 pound of pasta.

About 1½ cups; for pasta for 6. About 115 calories each.

Lower-Calorie Basil Sauce

Pesto III

3 cups tightly packed basil
   leaves
2 teaspoons chopped garlic
2 tablespoons chopped lemon
   rind
3 tablespoons chopped Italian
   parsley

1 teaspoon salt
¼ teaspoon pepper
2 tablespoons olive oil
¼ cup ricotta cheese

Put all of the ingredients into a blender or food processor and blend until smooth. Use ½ cup mixed with 2 tablespoons of water to 1 pound of pasta.

About 1¼ cups, for pasta for 6. About 65 calories each.

Spinach Pesto Sauce

Pesto con Spinaci

2 pounds fresh spinach,
   chopped (about 3 cups)
2 teaspoons dried basil
1 cup chopped Italian parsley
¼ cup pine nuts (*pignoli*)

2 cloves garlic, chopped
3 tablespoons olive oil
3 tablespoons grated
   Parmesan or Romano
   cheese

This sauce is made when fresh basil is not available.

Bring the spinach to a boil and drain. Follow the directions for Basil Sauce I*.

About 1 cup; sauce for 6. About 140 calories each.

Eggs

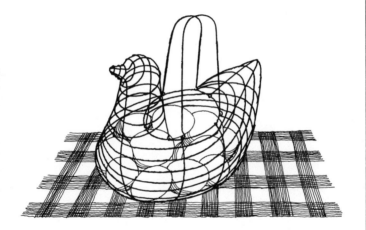

IN ITALY, EGGS are seldom served for breakfast; they are used as a main course for a light meal — luncheon or supper — and they may become the first course of a dinner. Eggs are often combined with vegetables. Italian scrambled eggs are similar to American ones, but Italian omelets — *frittata* — are different. We make French omelets, which are soft in the middle and are folded into an oval shape, and occasionally we make the soufflé type of omelet. Italian ones, however, while not dry, are firm, open-faced, and resemble large pancakes. If you're skillful, you can flip one over as you would a pancake; otherwise, turn it out on a warm plate and reverse it back into the pan or — and this is the easiest — brown the top for a minute under the broiler. Italian fried eggs, *uova al burro,* are what we call shirred eggs; and the poached eggs are usually cooked in a sauce or broth, although water or even an egg poacher are sometimes used. Northern Italian cooks prefer butter, while Southern ones like olive oil; you may substitute oil (or margarine) for butter in any of the following recipes, but, of course, use only as little as possible. As in any low-calorie cooking, you must use fats sparingly.

Servings and calories are given for main course for luncheon or light supper.

Poached Eggs in Broth

Uova Affogate in Brodo

1½ cups chicken broth
juice of ½ lemon
¼ teaspoon salt

4 eggs
4 pieces toast
minced parsley (garnish)

Heat the broth with lemon juice and salt. When it is simmering, slip in the eggs carefully and cook until the white is set. Be careful not to overcook. Remove with a slotted spoon and serve on toast sprinkled with parsley, if you wish.

Serves 2. About 160 calories without toast; about 60 calories extra for each slice of toast.

Eggs Poached in Tomato Sauce

Uova con Salsa di Pomidoro

2 cups tomato sauce
3 leaves fresh chopped or
  1 teaspoon dried basil

6 eggs

Heat the tomato sauce with the basil. When bubbly, slip in the eggs. If the pan is not large enough, do in two lots. The eggs may float; if so, spoon the boiling sauce over. Cook only until the white is set. Remove to a hot plate and serve with the sauce poured over.

Serves 6. About 150 calories each.

Eggs Poached in Tomato-Basil Sauce

Uova al Piatto coi Pomidori e Basilico

2 tablespoons broth
1 small onion, minced
1 pound canned or fresh
  Italian plum tomatoes,
  peeled and chopped

1 teaspoon salt
¼ teaspoon pepper
2 tablespoons fresh minced or
  1 teaspoon dried basil
6 eggs

Preheat oven to 350°.

Heat the broth in a skillet; add the onion and cook gently for a minute. Do not brown. Add the tomatoes with their juice, salt, pepper, and basil. Simmer for 15 minutes until reduced and thickened. Transfer to 6 individual ovenproof dishes. Drop an egg into each, spoon a little of the sauce over, and bake until the whites are set, about 6 or 7 minutes. This makes a good first course.

Serves 6. About 140 calories each.

Eggs in Tomato Sauce

Uova al Pomidoro Fresco

1 medium onion, chopped
1 tablespoon olive oil
3 cups peeled, chopped fresh
    tomatoes
1 teaspoon salt

¼ teaspoon pepper
½ teaspoon oregano
8 eggs
4 pieces of toast, cut in half

Sauté the onions in the oil until transparent. Add the tomatoes and seasonings and simmer, uncovered, for 10 minutes, stirring frequently. Slip in the eggs one at a time, spoon the sauce over, and cook only until the whites are set. Serve the eggs on toast with the sauce poured over.

Serves 8. About 160 calories each.

Eggs Hunter's Style

Uova alla Cacciatora

6 chicken livers, cut in half
2 tablespoons minced onion
1 tablespoon olive oil
2 tablespoons broth
½ cup tomato purée

2 tablespoons white wine
1 teaspoon salt
¼ teaspoon pepper
8 eggs

Sauté the chicken livers and onion in the oil for 2 minutes in a large skillet. Add the broth and simmer for 2 minutes. Add the tomato purée mixed with the wine and the salt and pepper and simmer, uncovered, for 5 minutes. Slide in the eggs carefully, one at a time. Cover and cook until the whites are set, about 2 minutes.

Serves 6. About 190 calories each.

Scrambled Eggs with Peppers

Uova con Peperoni

1 large green pepper   ½ teaspoon salt
1 tablespoon olive oil   ¼ teaspoon pepper
6 eggs

Seed the pepper and cut into thin stripes about ¾ inch long. Sauté in the oil for 3 or 4 minutes; cover and cook for 15 minutes, adding a little water. The strips should be soft. Beat the eggs with salt and pepper and pour over the pepper strips. Cook and stir until the eggs are set but not too firm. Remove at once from the pan, or they will continue to cook.

Serves 4. About 165 calories each.

Scrambled Eggs with Tomatoes

Uova con Pomidori

1 tablespoon butter   6 eggs
2 fresh tomatoes, peeled and   ½ teaspoon salt
   chopped, or 1 cup canned   ¼ teaspoon pepper
   Italian plum tomatoes,
   chopped

Melt the butter in a skillet, add the tomatoes, and simmer for 5 minutes. Beat the eggs with the salt and pepper and pour over the tomatoes. Cook over low heat, while stirring, until the eggs are set but not too dry.

Serves 4. About 150 calories each.

Scrambled Eggs with Ricotta Cheese

Uova con Ricotta

¼ pound skim-milk ricotta
  cheese
3 tablespoons buttermilk
1 tablespoon olive oil

6 eggs, beaten
1 teaspoon salt
2 tablespoons sherry

Smooth the cheese with buttermilk and heat it in a skillet or chafing dish. Stir in the oil, eggs, and salt, and stir and cook gently until the mixture is set and creamy. Stir in the sherry.

Serves 4. About 180 calories each.

Scrambled Eggs with Cheese

Uova Stracciati al Formaggio

6 eggs
1 tablespoon butter
½ teaspoon salt

¼ teaspoon pepper
2 tablespoons grated
  Parmesan cheese

Beat the eggs with a fork only until the yolks and whites are blended. Melt the butter in a pan; when it foams, pour in the eggs. Stir steadily while cooking. Be careful not to let the eggs get dry; they continue to cook after you turn off the heat. Season with salt and pepper. Put into a hot serving dish or 4 plates and sprinkle with the cheese.

Serves 4. About 180 calories each.

Scrambled Eggs with Mushrooms

Uovo con Funghi

1 small onion, chopped
3 tablespoons broth
⅓ pound mushrooms, sliced
1 tablespoon minced parsley

8 eggs
1 teaspoon salt
¼ teaspoon pepper

Melt the butter and brown the onion in the broth for 2 minutes. Add the mushrooms and parsley and cook gently for 2 minutes. Meanwhile, beat the eggs with the salt and pepper and pour over the onion-mushroom mixture. Stir until the eggs are set but soft and remove at once to serving plates.

Serves 6. About 130 calories each.

Basic Omelet

Frittata

6 eggs	2 tablespoons water or milk
¼ teaspoon salt	2 tablespoons butter
pinch white pepper	

Beat the eggs, salt, pepper, and water or milk, using a fork. (Water makes a more delicate omelet.) Melt the butter in a hot omelet pan; when it foams, pour in the eggs. Do not brown the butter. Lower the heat and stir with one hand while shaking the pan with the other. Lift the edges of the omelet with the fork and let the loose portions run under. When the eggs are almost set, turn off the heat, stop stirring, and let the omelet rest for 1 minute.

Turn it out onto a hot platter or plate. Put it back to brown the other side or serve it brown side up, as it is in the platter. Instead of turning it out, you may brown it for a minute under the broiler.

Serves 3. About 220 calories each.

Cheese Omelet

Frittata al Formaggio

10 eggs	½ teaspoon salt
3 tablespoons grated	¼ teaspoon pepper
Parmesan cheese	2 tablespoons butter
3 tablespoons water	

Beat the eggs with the cheese, water, salt, and pepper. Heat the butter; when it foams, pour in the egg mixture. Stir, lifting the edges to let the uncooked egg run under. When the eggs are almost set, stop stirring and let the omelet sit for 1 minute. Turn and brown or fold over or run under the broiler for 1 minute or less to heat the top.

Serves 6. About 200 calories each.

Mushroom Omelet

Frittata di Funghi

½ pound mushrooms, sliced
2 tablespoons butter
½ teaspoon salt

½ clove garlic, crushed
1 tablespoon chopped parsley
8 eggs

Sauté the mushrooms in the butter with all the remaining ingredients except the eggs. Cook gently for 3 minutes. Turn down the heat and let the mushrooms rest and give their juice. Beat the eggs and pour over the mushrooms. Stir gently and lift the edges to let the uncooked egg run under. When the bottom is light brown, turn and brown the other side or run it under the broiler for 1 minute.

Serves 6. About 160 calories each.

Onion Omelet

Frittata di Cipolla

1 large Bermuda onion, sliced
   very thin
2 tablespoons oil

4 eggs
½ teaspoon salt
¼ teaspoon pepper

Sauté the onion in 1 tablespoon of the oil very gently until limp but not brown, about 3 minutes. Remove to a bowl and add the eggs, salt, and pepper and beat together. Heat the remaining oil in the skillet and add the egg-onion mixture. Stir for 1 minute, then let cook slowly for 3 minutes until brown underneath. Turn and brown the other side. If you can't turn it, cut it in half or into quarters to turn or brown it for 1 minute under the broiler.

Serves 3. About 190 calories each.

Zucchini Omelet

Frittata di Zucchini

1 small onion, sliced thin	½ teaspoon salt
2 tablespoons oil	¼ teaspoon pepper
4 medium zucchini, sliced ¼ inch thick	1 tablespoon minced parsley
8 eggs	3 tablespoons grated Parmesan cheese (optional)

Sauté the onion in the oil until transparent. Add the zucchini and brown lightly.

Meanwhile, beat the eggs with the salt, pepper, and parsley. Add the onion-zucchini mixture to the eggs and blend thoroughly. Return to the skillet, adding a little oil or butter if necessary.

Cook slowly while stirring for a minute, then let it cook until the bottom is very lightly browned. Run it under the broiler for 1 minute to set. This omelet must not be brown. Sprinkle with cheese if you wish.

Serves 6. About 180 calories each without cheese.

Omelet with Onions and Tomatoes

Frittata di Cipolle e Pomidori

1 large sweet onion, slivered	6 eggs, beaten
2 tablespoons olive oil	salt and pepper
1 cup peeled chopped tomatoes	¼ teaspoon sugar

Sauté the onion in the oil until light brown. Add the tomatoes, salt, pepper, and sugar and simmer for 10 minutes to reduce the moisture. Stir in the eggs and cook gently while stirring until the eggs start to become firm, then leave for a minute until set but not dry. Turn out onto a hot plate with the brown side up.

Serves 4. About 200 calories each.

Omelet with Meat and Vegetables

Frittata di Verdura e Carne

1 medium onion, sliced thin	8 eggs, beaten
2 tablespoons olive oil	salt
1 cup chopped cooked meat	
1½ cups chopped cooked vegetables	

Sauté the onion in the oil until light brown. Add the meat, which can be one kind or a mixture. The vegetables can be any leftovers. Add to the pan and stir over low heat for about 5 minutes. Remove from the heat, stir in the eggs, and taste for seasoning. The amount of salt to be added depends on the seasonings in the cooked food.

Cook and stir until the eggs are almost set, then let omelet cook gently until brown underneath and not too dry on top. Brown the other side by turning or running it under the broiler.

Serves 6. About 225 calories each.

Basic Shirred Eggs

Uova alla Coccote

4 tablespoons milk	¼ teaspoon pepper
8 eggs	½ teaspoon minced parsley
½ teaspoon salt	(garnish)

Preheat oven to 375°.

Put 1 tablespoon of the milk in each of 4 shirred-egg dishes (flat ramekins) and slip 2 eggs into each. Sprinkle with salt and pepper and the parsley. Bake until the whites are set, 6 to 8 minutes. Serve in the dishes.

Serves 4. About 170 calories each.

Shirred Eggs with Ham

Uova in Tazzini con Prosciutto

2 tablespoons butter
4 teaspoons chopped ham
4 tablespoons milk

8 eggs
1 teaspoon salt
½ teaspoon white pepper

Preheat oven to 350°.

Butter 4 heatproof individual baking dishes, using about half of the butter. Put 1 teaspoon of ham and 1 tablespoon of milk into each. Put 2 eggs into each dish, sprinkle with salt and pepper, and top with the remaining butter. Bake in a hot water bath until the whites are set, about 7 or 8 minutes.

Serves 4. About 250 calories each.

Shirred Eggs with Chicken Livers

Uova con Fegatini

½ cup milk
8 eggs
1 teaspoon salt
¼ teaspoon pepper

¼ pound chicken livers, cut up
2 tablespoons butter

Preheat oven to 350°.

Put a little milk in each of 4 ramekins. Slip 2 eggs into each; sprinkle with salt and pepper. Bake for about 10 minutes. Meanwhile, sauté the chicken livers in butter for several minutes and add to the half-cooked eggs. Cook only until the whites are set.

Serves 4. About 275 calories each.

Shirred Eggs with Cheese

Uova alla Coccote con Formaggio

6 teaspoons butter	12 eggs
2 ounces Fontina or	1 teaspoon salt
Mozzarella cheese, diced	

Preheat oven to 400°.

Put a teaspoon of butter into 6 medium or large ramekins or shirred-egg dishes. Sprinkle the cheese over the butter and heat in the oven until the cheese melts. Put 2 eggs into each dish. Sprinkle with the salt. Bake until the whites are set, about 8 minutes.

Serves 6. About 220 calories each.

Fish

THE ADRIATIC and the Mediterranean offer a treasure of sea fare — *frutte di mare* — and we are not far behind with the fruits of our seas. A variety of fish is available in most markets, which makes it easy for us to use several kinds of fish, rather than just one, in many of our fish soups and entrées. This adds to the interest without adding to the cost or calories.

One rule applies to all fish cooking: do not overcook. Fish is delicate and should be cooked slowly and for a short time; it is easy to wait until it is so soft that it is almost impossible to serve and is tasteless. Test it with a fork; if it flakes, it is done. Don't overseason or oversauce fish.

Fish is not only good and good for you, it has comparatively few calories. A smart Italian calorie-conscious cook will specialize in fish dishes.

Broiled Fish Fillets

Filetti di Pesce alla Griglia

6 fillets of cod, haddock, trout, or flounder (about 2 pounds)
½ teaspoon paprika
½ teaspoon salt
½ teaspoon pepper
3 tablespoons melted butter or part olive oil, part butter
2 tablespoons lemon juice

Preheat broiler.

Sprinkle the fillets with the paprika, salt, and pepper.

Combine the butter and lemon juice and brush over the fish. Place on a broiler rack and broil for 4 minutes, brush again, turn, brush, and broil for 3 minutes. Serve with any remaining butter and lemon mixture poured over.

Serves 6. About 180 calories each.

Poached Fish Fillets

Pesce Lesso

1 tablespoon minced parsley
1 tablespoon minced fresh or 1 teaspoon dried dill
¼ teaspoon oregano
1 teaspoon salt
¼ teaspoon pepper

1½ cups broth: fish, clam, or chicken
2 pounds flounder or haddock fillets
2 tablespoons butter
1 teaspoon lemon juice

Add the parsley, dill, oregano, salt, and pepper to the broth; bring to a boil and simmer gently for about 3 minutes. Slip in the fish fillets and simmer gently for about 7 minutes. Remove carefully so as not to break them.

Melt the butter, add the lemon juice and ¼ cup of the fish broth, and pour over.

Serves 6. About 170 calories each.

Fish Fillets in White Vermouth

Filetti di Pesce in Vermut

6 fish fillets: sole, flounder, turbot, or cod, about ⅓ pound each
3 tablespoons chopped scallions or chives

1 teaspoon lemon juice
½ teaspoon salt
½ teaspoon white pepper
½ cup dry vermouth

Preheat oven to 350°.

Put the fillets in one row in a shallow baking dish.

Sprinkle with scallions or chives or a mixture of the two. Add the lemon juice, salt, and pepper, and pour the wine over. Bake for 30 minutes.

Serves 6. About 150 calories each.

Fillets of Sole with Parmesan Cheese

Sogliola alla Parmigiana

1½ pounds fillets of sole	2 tablespoons grated
½ teaspoon salt	Parmesan cheese
flour	¼ cup chicken broth
2 tablespoons butter	minced parsley (garnish)

Sprinkle the sole with the salt, dust with the flour, and sauté in the butter for 5 minutes, turning once to brown evenly. Sprinkle with the cheese and add the broth. Cover and simmer for 5 minutes. Serve sprinkled with parsley.

Serves 4. About 240 calories each.

Fish Fillets with Tomato Sauce

Filetti di Pesce al Sugo

2 pounds fish fillets: flounder,	1 tablespoon butter
haddock, halibut, or sole	¼ pound mushrooms, sliced
3 tablespoons chopped onion	1 can (6 ounces) tomato sauce

Preheat oven to 350°.

Put the fillets in a greased flat baking dish, preferably Pyrex. Sauté the onions in the butter for 3 or 4 minutes; add the mushrooms and sauté for 2 minutes more. Add the tomato sauce, stir, and pour over the fillets. Bake for about 30 minutes.

Serves 6. About 160 calories each.

Fish Fillets with Orange

Filetti di Pesce col Aranci

¼ pound mushrooms, sliced
2 scallions, minced
2 tablespoons oil or melted
  margarine
3 tablespoons frozen orange
  juice concentrate or 6
  tablespoons orange juice

½ cup white wine
½ teaspoon salt
¼ teaspoon pepper
2 pounds fish fillets: sole or
  flounder
6 thin orange slices (garnish)

Preheat oven to 350°.

Sauté the mushrooms and scallions in the oil or margarine for 3 minutes. Add the thawed orange juice concentrate or orange juice, wine, salt, and pepper and stir. Place the fillets in a greased shallow baking dish and pour the mixture over. The liquid should almost cover the fish; if it doesn't, add more wine. Bake for 30 minutes.

It's easier to serve right from the baking dish. Garnish with orange slices.

Serves 6. About 195 calories each.

Spicy Fish Fillets

Filetti di Pesce con Salsa Piccante

1½ pounds fresh or frozen fish
  fillets
paprika
1 cup yogurt
½ teaspoon prepared mustard
½ teaspoon dried dill and/or
  thyme

1 tablespoon lemon juice
1 teaspoon salt
½ teaspoon pepper
minced parsley (garnish)

Preheat oven to 350°.

If using frozen fish, thaw. Cut into 2 pieces and dust with paprika. Grease a small baking dish and lay the fish in it. Combine the yogurt, mustard, dill and/or thyme, lemon juice, salt, and pepper. Blend well and spread over the fish. Bake for 20 minutes. Sprinkle with parsley.

Serves 4. About 200 calories each.

Fillets of Sole or Flounder in Parchment or Foil

Filetti di Sogliole al Cartoccio

2 cups torn lettuce	4 teaspoons butter
1½ pounds fillet of sole or flounder	1 teaspoon salt
	¼ teaspoon pepper
2 scallions, slivered	½ teaspoon dill weed or basil
2 tomatoes, peeled and chopped	4 teaspoons white wine

Preheat oven to 350°.

Cut brown paper or foil into 4 large squares. Put a small amount of lettuce in each and cover with the fish, dividing the fillets evenly. Combine the remaining ingredients and divide among the fish squares. Wrap the fish envelope fashion, so no moisture will escape.

Place on a baking sheet and bake for about 35 minutes. Serve in the packages so each may empty the fish and all the juices onto his or her plate.

Serves 4. About 160 calories each.

Fish Fillets in Foil

Filetti al Cartoccio

4 fillets of sole or flounder, 1½ to 2 pounds total	1 tablespoon flour
	1 teaspoon salt
¼ teaspoon minced scallions or onions	¼ teaspoon pepper
	1 tablespoon white or red wine or vinegar
2 tablespoons butter	

Preheat oven to 350°.

Place each piece of fish on a square of foil large enough

to wrap the fish in. Sauté the scallions or onions in the butter until transparent, not brown. Sprinkle with flour, salt, and pepper, stir in the wine or vinegar, and place a portion of this on each fillet. Wrap envelope-fashion and bake for about 30 minutes.

Serves 4. About 240 calories each.

Small Fish in Foil

Pesce al Cartoccio

6 fish such as trout, perch, small mackerel, or large smelt (about ⅓ to ½ pound each)	3 scallions, sliced lengthwise
	6 small sprigs parsley
	6 tablespoons butter
	2 tablespoons lemon juice
spinach or lettuce leaves	1 teaspoon salt

Preheat oven to 375°.

Leave the heads and tails on the fish. Place each fish and a few spinach or lettuce leaves on a square of foil large enough to wrap around it. Add some of the scallions, parsley, butter, lemon juice, salt, and a few more leaves to each square. Wrap tight, envelope-fashion. Bake for 30 minutes. Serve in the foil so that each will open his or her own and have all the juice on the plate.

Serves 6. About 230 calories each.

Broiled Fish Steaks

Trance di Pesce alla Griglia

1½ pounds fish steaks: halibut, bass, or red snapper	¼ teaspoon paprika
	1 tablespoon minced parsley
2 tablespoons dry vermouth	1 teaspoon rosemary
2 teaspoons prepared mustard	lemon wedges
½ teaspoon salt	

Preheat broiler.

Cut the fish into serving-size pieces. Combine all the

remaining ingredients (except the lemon wedges) and spread half over the fish. Turn the fish and spread with the remaining mixture. Broil for 5 minutes, baste with the pan juices; turn, brush again, and broil 5 minutes more. Remove to a serving dish, pouring any juices over. Serve with the lemon wedges.

Serves 4. About 150 calories each.

Broiled Fish Steaks with Garlic-Lemon Sauce

Pesce all'Agliata e Limone

4 fish steaks (any fish), about
  1½ to 2 pounds total
2 tablespoons bread crumbs
2 cloves garlic, crushed or
  minced

2 tablespoons lemon juice
½ teaspoon salt
¼ teaspoon paprika
2 tablespoons olive oil

Preheat broiler.

Broil the steaks for about 5 minutes on each side. Meanwhile, make the sauce. Combine the crumbs, garlic, lemon juice, salt, and paprika and mix well; add the oil gradually, while stirring, to make a thick creamy mixture. Serve the fish topped with the sauce.

Serves 4. About 215 calories each.

Broiled Fish

Pesce alla Griglia

2 pounds fish steaks or whole
  fish (haddock, halibut, cod,
  or perch)
2 tablespoons olive oil
2 tablespoons lemon juice

1 teaspoon salt
¼ teaspoon pepper
2 tablespoons minced parsley
2 teaspoons basil or rosemary

Preheat broiler.

Brush the fish with a mixture of oil and lemon juice and place on a broiler pan. Combine the remaining ingredients and sprinkle half of the mixture on the fish. Broil for 4 to 6 minutes, depending on the thickness of the fish.   Brush with oil and lemon juice, turn, and brush again. Sprinkle with the remaining herb mixture and broil for 4 or 5 minutes. Be careful when turning and serving the fish; it breaks easily.

Serves 4. About 225 calories each.

Poached Cod Fillets

Filetti di Baccalà

2 tablespoons wine, red or
  white
1 cup water
1 teaspoon minced parsley or
  2 teaspoons dried parsley
  flakes
2 tablespoons minced onion

¼ teaspoon sugar
½ teaspoon pepper
½ teaspoon thyme
1 teaspoon lemon juice
2½ pounds cod fillets
  (haddock or flounder may be
  substituted)

Preheat oven to 350°.

Put all of the ingredients except the fish into a baking dish and mix. Place the fish in this marinade and refrigerate for several hours. Put the baking dish in the oven, covered with a lid or foil, and bake for about 20 minutes, or simmer gently on top of the stove. Uncover and cook about 15 minutes more.

Serves 6. About 175 calories each.

Stuffed Fillets Poached in White Wine

Filetti di Pesce in Vino Bianco

2 tablespoons minced
  scallions or shallots
3 tablespoons margarine
⅓ pound mushrooms, sliced
  thin
2 teaspoons minced parsley

½ teaspoon pepper
1 teaspoon salt
6 fillets of sole or flounder,
  about 2¼ pounds total
½ cup dry white wine

Sauté the scallions or shallots in 2 tablespoons of the margarine until limp. Add the mushrooms to the pan. Simmer and stir for 2 minutes, then add the parsley, pepper, and ½ teaspoon of the salt.

Place the fillets flat on a board and spread with the mushroom mixture. Don't put on too much, and don't put it near the edges. Roll the fillets and fasten with toothpicks. Sprinkle with remaining salt.

Place in a greased shallow baking dish and pour the wine over. Cover with a lid or foil. Simmer for about 15 minutes (the wine should not boil).

When ready to serve, remove the toothpicks and serve in the baking dish; or transfer to a hot platter, remove the toothpicks, and pour the liquid over.

Serves 6. About 220 calories each.

Broiled Swordfish

Pesce Spada alla Griglia

1½ pounds swordfish cut about 1 inch thick
1 tablespoon lemon juice
1 tablespoon olive oil

1 clove garlic, crushed
1 teaspoon salt
¼ teaspoon paprika
lemon wedges

Preheat broiler.

Place the swordfish in a deep bowl. Combine the remaining ingredients (except the lemon wedges) and pour over the fish. Marinate for an hour. Broil close to the heat for 4 minutes, turn, and broil for 3 minutes on the other side. Baste with the marinade as the fish broils. Pour any remaining marinade over. Serve with lemon wedges.

Serves 4. About 220 calories each.

Baked Citrus Fish

Pesce col Limone al Forno

1½ to 2 pounds fish: halibut,
   red snapper, sea or striped
   bass, steaks or whole fish
¼ cup chopped onion
2 tablespoons chopped
   pimiento

1 tablespoon oil
2 tablespoons lemon juice
2 tablespoons orange juice
¼ teaspoon pepper
½ teaspoon seasoned salt

Preheat oven to 375°.

If using a whole fish, remove the head and tail. Sauté the onion and pimiento in the oil for 2 minutes. Add the fruit juices. Place the fish on top of the vegetables and sprinkle with pepper and salt. Bake for 30 minutes, basting with the pan juices several times. Remove the fish to a warm serving dish and pour the juices over.

Serves 4. About 190 calories each.

Baked Halibut

Pesce in Bianco al Forno I

2 pounds halibut
¼ teaspoon pepper
½ teaspoon paprika
1 clove garlic

3 tablespoons minced parsley
½ cup bread crumbs
1 lemon, cut into 6 slices

Preheat oven to 350°.

Place the fish in a shallow baking dish and sprinkle with the pepper and paprika. Squeeze the garlic over and sprinkle with parsley and bread crumbs. Place the lemon slices over the fish and add water almost to cover the fish. Bake uncovered for 45 minutes.

Serves 6. About 175 calories each.

Baked Haddock

Pesce in Bianco al Forno II

1½ pounds haddock
about 2 cups skim milk

1 tablespoon butter or olive oil
¼ teaspoon white pepper

Preheat oven to 375°.

Cut the haddock into serving pieces. Place in a lightly greased shallow baking dish. Pour the milk over and add the butter or oil and pepper. If the milk doesn't thoroughly cover the fish, add more. Bake for about 30 minutes; test for flakiness after 20 minutes. Serve from the dish.

Serves 4. About 190 calories each.

Baked Sea Bass

Spigola Arrosto

1 4-pound sea or striped bass
1 teaspoon salt
¼ teaspoon pepper
2 tablespoons butter, melted
1 tablespoon olive oil

1 tablespoon lemon juice
½ cup thinly sliced onions
  (optional)
lemon wedges

Preheat oven to 350°.

Wash the fish and pat dry; do not remove the head or tail. Make two diagonal slashes on each side of the fish. Sprinkle with the salt and pepper and place on a baking pan, ovenproof platter, or casserole on top of 1 tablespoon of the melted butter and the oil. Brush with the remaining butter and the lemon juice; spread with the onions, if you wish. Bake for 30 minutes; baste well with the juices in the pan. Continue to bake about 20 minutes more.

It is hard to lift the fish out in one piece, so be careful or serve it from the baking dish. Serve with lemon wedges.

Serves 6. About 200 calories each.

Trout with Mushrooms

Trota ai Funghi

½ pound mushrooms, sliced
  thin
1 teaspoon salt
4 small brook trout (about
  2 pounds)

1 tablespoon lemon juice
2 tablespoons butter

Preheat oven to 375°.

Put the mushrooms on the bottom of a buttered flat baking dish with ½ teaspoon of the salt. Place the trout on top of the mushrooms; sprinkle with the lemon juice and the remaining salt. Dot with the butter. Bake for 15 minutes. If the trout is not lightly browned on top, raise the heat to 500° for 3 or 4 minutes or put under the broiler for 2 minutes. Serve in the baking dish.

Serves 4. About 210 calories each.

Fish with Tomatoes

Pesce ai Pomidori

2½ pounds fish fillets or slices
1 teaspoon salt
¼ teaspoon pepper
2 tablespoons olive oil
1 clove garlic, crushed
3 tablespoons white wine
  vinegar

2 pounds fresh tomatoes,
  peeled and chopped, or 1
  can (2 pounds) peeled
  tomatoes
2 tablespoons minced parsley

Sprinkle the fish with the salt and pepper and brown on both sides in the oil, adding the garlic as you turn the fish. Add the vinegar and simmer for 2 minutes. Add the tomatoes and parsley, cover, and simmer for 20 minutes. Serve with the sauce poured over the fish.

Serves 6. About 240 calories each.

Pan-Broiled Mackerel

Sgomberi in Tegame

2 cloves garlic, minced
2 tablespoons olive oil
4 small mackerel
1 bay leaf, crushed

1 tablespoon lemon juice
½ teaspoon salt
¼ teaspoon pepper
lemon wedges

If oven is used, preheat to 350°.

Sauté the garlic in the oil for 2 minutes. Add the mackerel and brown lightly on both sides. Add the bay leaf, lemon juice, salt, and pepper. Cover and simmer very gently for 15 minutes, or bake for 20 minutes. Serve with the lemon wedges. Be careful not to break the fish when removing from the pan.

Serves 4. About 300 calories each.

Mackerel in White Wine

Sgomberi al Vino Bianco

6 small mackerel, about ½
  pound each
½ teaspoon dried or 1
  teaspoon chopped fresh
  rosemary

½ recipe white wine court
  bouillon
lemon wedges

Preheat oven to 350°.

Clean the mackerel and leave the heads and tails on; they add flavor to the liquid. Place the fish in a baking dish, add the rosemary, and pour the court bouillon over. It should come at least halfway up the fish; if not, add a little wine or water. Put into the oven and bake for 15 to 20 minutes after the liquid comes to a simmer — it must not boil. Serve from the baking dish, on a warm platter, or on individual plates with a little sauce poured over. Pass the lemon wedges.

Serves 6. About 255 calories each.

Poached Cod with Horseradish Sauce

Filetti di Baccalà in Bianco con Salsa

2 pounds cod in one piece or
  fillets or steaks
2 tablespoons butter
2 tablespoons flour
1 cup skim milk or ½ cup milk
  and ½ cup fish stock or clam
  broth

2 teaspoons freshly grated or 2
  tablespoons prepared
  horseradish
1 teaspoon lemon juice

Poach the cod in salted water for about 10 minutes or simmer in salted water for 12 minutes. Fillets will take less time than steaks or one large piece. Meanwhile, melt the butter, blend in the flour, and add the milk and fish broth while stirring. If using fresh horseradish, add and simmer until thickened. If using prepared, simmer sauce until thickened and then stir in the horseradish. Taste for seasoning. Serve the sauce on the side.

Serves 6. About 185 calories each.

Cold Salmon

Salmone Freddo con Maionese

2 pounds salmon steaks
2 tablespoons lemon juice
1 tablespoon minced parsley

1 teaspoon salt
lemon wedges (garnish)
low-calorie mayonnaise

Wrap the fish in cheesecloth and place in water to cover. Add the lemon juice, parsley, and salt. Simmer for 15 minutes. Place on a cold platter and remove the cheesecloth. Chill in the refrigerator for several hours. Garnish with lemon wedges and pass the mayonnaise.

Serves 6. About 225 calories each with diet mayonnaise.

Fish Stew I

Brodetto I

2 pounds assorted fish: cod,
   haddock, halibut, swordfish,
   bass, sole, or flounder
1 pound mussels
¼ cup chopped onion
2 tablespoons olive oil

1 clove garlic, minced
1 cup canned peeled Italian
   tomatoes
½ cup wine
½ pound shrimp, peeled
¼ cup chopped parsley

Cut the fish into serving pieces. Steam the mussels in ½ cup water; when they open, let stand until cool. Meanwhile, sauté the onion in the oil for 3 minutes; add the garlic and after a minute the undrained tomatoes, wine, and the liquid from the mussels. Add the fish and a little water, almost to cover the fish. Cover and simmer for about 15 minutes. Remove the mussels from their shells and add with the shrimp and parsley; simmer 3 minutes.
   Serves 6. About 260 calories each.

Fish Stew II

Brodetto II

2½ pounds assorted fish and
   shellfish
2 cloves garlic, minced
2 tablespoons olive oil
½ cup red wine
½ cup wine vinegar

½ teaspoon salt
¼ teaspoon pepper
¼ teaspoon red pepper
2 tablespoons minced parsley
6 slices bread or toast
   (optional)

Cut the large fish into serving pieces. The fish may be chosen from sole, mullet, halibut, or whiting; the shellfish, from clams, squid, lobster, shrimp, and mussels. Sauté the garlic in the oil for a minute. Add the larger pieces of fish, cook for a few minutes, and then add the smaller pieces, such as shrimp and clams. After a few minutes add the wine, vinegar, salt, pepper, and red pepper. Cover and cook gently for 15 minutes; add the parsley and stir. Serve on slices of bread or toast in soup plates.

Serves 6. About 225 calories each without bread; with bread add 60 calories.

Salt Codfish in Sauce

Baccalà al Sugo

1½ pounds dry salt codfish
2 medium onions, sliced thin
2 tablespoons olive oil
2 cups canned or fresh peeled
  plum tomatoes

3 tablespoons blanched raisins
½ teaspoon pepper

Soak the fish in cold water for 24 hours or longer, changing the water frequently. Clean it and cut it into serving pieces.

Sauté the onions in the oil until lightly browned; add the tomatoes and simmer for 10 minutes. Add the fish, raisins, and pepper and cook gently for 20 minutes. You probably won't need salt.

Serves 4. About 330 calories each.

Baked Eel

Anguille Arrostite

Eel is very popular in Italy; if you can get fresh eel, do cook it Italian style.

2½ pounds eel, skinned and
  sliced into 2-inch pieces
2 tablespoons flour
½ teaspoon salt
¼ teaspoon pepper

2 tablespoons oil
3 bay leaves
juice of 1 large lemon
lemon wedges

Preheat oven to 350°.

Dust the eel with flour, salt, and pepper. Brown it in the oil and drain on paper toweling. Place it in a baking dish or casserole with the bay leaves and lemon juice. Bake for 30 minutes. Serve with lemon wedges.

Serves 6. About 200 calories each.

Shellfish

THE WORD *scampi* has become synonymous with shrimp in languages all over the world, although the Italians use different names for the various types of this crustacean. Delicious as frozen shrimp are, they are even better fresh, which — thanks to aviation — is no longer limited to coastal areas. Mussels (*cozze*) are justifiably popular in Italy, and as they are just as good in this country, it seems strange that we don't eat more of them. The Mediterranean *aragosta* is a spiny lobster, similar to our Pacific ones, and cannot compete with the cherished creatures from the state of Maine. Oysters (*ostriche*) also benefit from cold water, and they are less popular in Italy than they are here. We can successfully substitute little neck or cherrystone clams for the small *vongole* or *arselle* of Italy.

Like fish, shellfish are a boon to dieters. They are a special treat, they make a meal memorable, and, with these streamlined recipes, leave you with a feeling of well-being and a clear conscience.

Boiled Shrimp

Scampi Bolliti

If serving the shrimp cold, boil in the shell and peel and devein after cooking. If serving them hot, shell and devein before.

2 pounds shrimp in shells, 1½ pounds shelled	2 quarts salted water or court bouillon

If you are near the sea, boil the shrimp in sea water; if not, add 1 tablespoon salt to 2 quarts of water. Bring the water to a boil, add the shrimp, and simmer for 2 minutes, until they turn pink. If they are small, remove them from the water; if large, leave them for a few minutes more. The secret of cooking shrimp is not to overcook them.

Serve cold with cocktail sauce or in a salad with ⅓ cup chopped celery and a low-calorie dressing. Serve hot with lemon wedges and pass melted butter for those who wish it.

Serves 4. About 135 calories each without butter.

Poached Shrimp in Soy-Curry Sauce

Scampi Bolliti con Salsa

2 tablespoons minced scallions or shallots	1 teaspoon salt
2 tablespoons vegetable oil	1 cup fish stock or clam juice
1 tablespoon curry powder	2 teaspoons cornstarch
1 teaspoon Worcestershire sauce	2 tablespoons water
	1¼ pounds shelled shrimp

Sauté the scallions or shallots in the oil until limp. Add the curry, Worcestershire sauce, salt, and fish stock. Cover and simmer for 6 to 9 minutes. Combine the cornstarch with the water and stir in. Boil while stirring until thickened and clear, about 2 minutes. Add the shrimp, bring to a rolling boil, cover, and shut off the heat. Let stand for about 5 minutes.

Serves 4. About 200 calories each.

Broiled Shrimp with Parsley

Scampi alla Griglia con Prezzemolo

2 pounds large shrimp	1 clove garlic, crushed
2 tablespoons olive oil	1 teaspoon lemon juice
¼ cup minced parsley	½ teaspoon pepper

Shell and devein the shrimp. Combine the remaining ingredients and pour over the shrimp. Refrigerate in the marinade for several hours.

Preheat broiler.

Place the shrimp in a broiler pan or on foil on the rack and broil about 5 inches from the heat for 3 minutes. Baste, turn, baste again, and broil for 2 minutes more.

Serves 4. About 190 calories each.

Broiled Shrimp with Whiskey

Scampi alla Griglia con Whiskey

2 pounds peeled and deveined large shrimp	2 tablespoons lemon juice
2 tablespoons melted butter	¼ cup whiskey

Preheat broiler.

Split the shrimp halfway through the long way and spread open. Place in a foil-lined broiler pan; pour over half the butter mixed with the lemon juice. Broil close to the heat for 3 mintues, baste, pour over 2 tablespoons of the whiskey, turn, brush with the remaining butter, and broil for 2 more minutes, basting two or three times. Serve with any remaining liquid poured over.

Serves 6. About 190 calories each.

Broiled Shrimp with Oil and Lemon and Garlic

Scampi all'Olio e Limone

1½ pounds shrimp	2 cloves garlic, crushed
3 tablespoons olive oil	½ teaspoon salt
2 tablespoons lemon juice	¼ teaspoon pepper

Peel the shrimp, leaving the tails on. Combine the remaining ingredients in a bowl. Place the shrimp in the marinade and refrigerate for several hours, turning the shrimp two or three times.

Preheat broiler. Place the shrimp in a broiler pan or on foil. Broil for 2 minutes close to the heat. Brush with the marinade, turn, brush again, and broil for 3 minutes. Baste again and serve with a little of the marinade poured over.

Serves 4. About 190 calories each.

Broiled Shrimp on a Skewer

Spiedini di Gamberi

2½ pounds medium shrimp	½ teaspoon salt
1 tablespoon olive oil	¼ teaspoon paprika
¼ cup vermouth or white wine	¼ cup minced parsley
1 clove garlic, crushed (optional)	lemon wedges (garnish)

Peel and devein the shrimp. Combine the remaining ingredients and marinate the shrimp for 2 to 3 hours.

Preheat broiler. String the shrimp lengthwise on 6 long skewers. (Curl each shrimp so the skewer will go through twice. This prevents their hanging down.) Place on the rack of a broiler pan and spoon a little marinade over. Broil for 5 minutes. Turn, baste with the marinade and pan juices, and broil for 3 more minutes.

Serves 6. About 160 calories each.

Shrimp with Almonds

Scampi con Màndorle

⅓ cup slivered almonds
1 tablespoon butter or
  margarine
2½ pounds shrimp, shelled
  and deveined

¼ teaspoon pepper
salt (optional)
2 tablespoons chopped chives
  or minced scallions

Sauté the almonds in the butter or margarine until light brown. Remove with a slotted spoon and drain. Sauté the shrimp in the same pan, stirring constantly, for 3 minutes. Sprinkle with the pepper and a little salt, if you wish. Sprinkle with the almonds and chives or scallions and serve at once.

Serves 6. About 220 calories each.

Shrimp Divan

Scampi con Asparagi

1½ pounds asparagus
1¾ pounds fresh or 2
  packages (10 ounces each)
  frozen shrimp
2 tablespoons margarine

2 tablespoons flour
1 cup skim milk
4 tablespoons shredded Swiss
  cheese

Preheat oven to 400°.

Cut the tough ends off the asparagus and scrape the stems up a few inches. Steam or cook in salted water. Drain and place in a greased shallow baking dish, preferably Pyrex.

Put the shrimp in water barely to cover in a saucepan, bring to a boil, and cook for 1 minute. Remove the shrimp and boil the liquid to reduce to about 3 tablespoons. When cool enough to handle, peel and devein the shrimp. Place them over the asparagus.

Melt the margarine, blend in the flour, and stir in the milk slowly. Simmer until thickened. Add the shrimp liquid and the cheese. Cook, stirring, until the cheese

melts. Pour over the shrimp and bake for 15 to 20 minutes, then put under the broiler for 3 or 4 minutes.
   Serves 6. About 210 calories each.

Shrimp with Scallions

Scampi Piccànte

5 scallions, sliced	1 teaspoon MSG
2 tablespoons vegetable oil, preferably peanut	1 cup clam broth or juice
	2 teaspoons cornstarch
1 teaspoon curry powder	2 tablespoons water
2 tablespoons soy sauce	1½ pounds medium shrimp

Sauté the scallions in the oil; add the curry, soy, MSG, and clam broth. Cover and simmer for 5 minutes. Combine the cornstarch and water and stir in. Cook until clear and thickened, about 2 minutes.
   Meanwhile, peel and devein the shrimp. If they are large, cut once through the center lengthwise; if small, leave them whole. Add the shrimp, bring to a boil, reduce the heat, and cook for 3 minutes, no more. Add more soy and curry to taste. The curry taste should not predominate.
   Serves 4. About 175 calories each.

Mussels with Rice

Cozze al Riso

3 pounds mussels	1 pound tomatoes, peeled
1 cup water	½ cup rice
2 cloves garlic, crushed	

Scrub and debeard the mussels; put them into a large pot with the water and garlic. Cover and cook until the mussels open — a few minutes only. When they are cool enough to handle, remove the mussels from their shells and, saving all the liquid, put the mussels aside. Transfer the liquid to a clean pan. Be careful not to pour in any sand that may be in the bottom of the large pot.

Meanwhile, purée the tomatoes in a blender or food processor or put through a food mill. Add the tomato purée and the rice to the mussel liquid. Simmer for 15 minutes, until the rice is tender; then add the mussels and reheat them.

Serves 4. About 225 calories each.

Mussels Steamed in Wine

Cozze al Vino

4 pounds mussels	3 tablespoons minced parsley
1 tablespoon oil	2 cloves garlic, minced
½ cup white or red wine	1 teaspoon oregano or basil

Scrub and debeard the mussels. Put into a large pot with the remaining ingredients. Cover and cook until the mussels open, about 7 or 8 minutes after the liquid has come to a boil. Serve with the liquid in soup plates, being careful to leave behind any sand that may have collected in the bottom of the pot.

Serves 4. About 180 calories each.

Boiled Lobster

Aragosta Bollita

4 live lobsters, 1 pound each	¼ cup vinegar
2 tablespoons salt	margarine, melted butter, or
4 sprigs parsley	olive oil
1 medium onion, chopped	lemon wedges
celery leaves	

METHOD 1. Place the live lobsters in a large pot of cold water. Add the salt, parsley, onion, celery leaves, and

vinegar and bring slowly to a boil. Cook for 10 minutes after the water has come to a boil. It is said by some that the lobsters are lulled to sleep as the water heats and do not have the shock of being plunged into boiling water, which perhaps toughens the flesh.

METHOD 2. Put the live lobsters, head first, into a pot of boiling water containing the salt, parsley, onion, celery leaves, and vinegar. If you can't bear to throw the lively lobsters into the hot water, put them into a large brown paper bag with holes in it and throw in the bag. Cook them for 12 to 15 minutes after the water comes back to a rolling boil and remove at once. Or, if they are to be served cold, cook for 10 minutes and let them cool in the liquid.

Split them down the center and crack the claws. If serving them cold, you may offer mayonnaise; if hot, melted margarine or butter or olive oil. Either hot or cold, pass the lemon wedges.

Serves 4. About 115 calories each without mayonnaise, butter, or oil.

Broiled Lobster

Aragosta alla Griglia

4 lobsters, 1 to 1¼ pounds
  each
2 tablespoons lemon juice
4 tablespoons melted butter or
  margarine

lemon wedges
melted butter (optional)

If you don't know how to kill a lobster, have the fish man do it. Cook immediately.

Preheat broiler.

Bend the lobster tails backward to crack the shell and make them lie flat, otherwise they will curl up as they broil. Place in a flat pan shell side down, sprinkle with the lemon juice, and brush with the melted butter or margarine. Broil about 5 inches from the heat for about

10 minutes, until the flesh turns white and is lightly browned and the shells are red. Serve with lemon wedges and pass extra melted butter to the nondieters.

Serves 4. About 220 calories each without extra butter.

Broiled Lobster with Brandy

Aragosta al Brandy

3 lobsters, about 1½ pounds each	2 tablespoons melted butter
	6 tablespoons brandy

Preheat broiler.

Split the lobsters and remove the sac behind each head. If you don't like to split live lobsters, have the fish man do it just before you cook them.

Place on the broiler pan shell side down, with a teaspoon of melted butter on each lobster tail. Broil until the lobster turns pink and the shells red, about 12 minutes.

Warm the brandy in a small saucepan. Place a half lobster on each plate, bring the brandy to the table, ignite, and pour a flaming tablespoonful over each half lobster.

Serves 6. About 145 calories each.

Deviled Lobster

Aragosta Fra Diavolo

2 lobsters, 2 pounds each, split	2 teaspoons oregano
1 clove garlic, minced	¼ teaspoon crushed red
2 tablespoons olive oil	pepper seeds or a generous
1 pound canned Italian tomatoes	pinch red pepper
	½ teaspoon salt
2 tablespoons minced parsley	¼ teaspoon pepper

Preheat oven to 375°.

Remove the small sac behind the head of the lobsters and the dark vein that runs down the tail. Leave any of the green part (tamale) or red (coral).

Place the lobsters, shell side down, in a baking pan. Sauté the garlic for a minute in the oil. Add the remaining ingredients and simmer together for 10 minutes. Pour over the lobsters and bake for about 15 to 20 minutes.

Serves 4. About 180 calories each.

Stuffed Squid

Calamari Ripiene

2 pounds small squid	¼ cup bread crumbs
½ cup chopped Italian parsley	2 tablespoons olive oil
1 tablespoon minced onion	wine, broth, or water
1 clove garlic, minced	

Preheat oven to 400°.

Cut or peel off the squid tentacles and set aside. Discard the eyes and the entrails from inside the squid. Peel off the outer skin while holding under running water.

Wash the tentacles thoroughly and chop them. Combine them with the parsley, onion, and garlic. Moisten the crumbs with the oil and add; stir well.

Stuff the bodies with this mixture but do not fill too full: the squid will shrink; the stuffing, swell. Fasten at the front with toothpicks stuck in from the top.

Place in one layer in a shallow pan with 1 inch of liquid — the wine, broth, or water — and bake for 30 minutes. The squid will puff up and look quite plump.

Remove the toothpicks. You may serve from the baking dish.

Serves 6. About 175 calories each.

Stuffed Baby Squid

Calamari Imbottiti

2½ pounds small squid
1 onion, minced
1 clove garlic, crushed
2 tablespoons olive oil
3 tablespoons parsley,
   chopped fine

1 teaspoon lemon juice
1 cup cooked rice
½ teaspoon salt
½ teaspoon oregano
1 large tomato
½ cup broth

Preheat oven to 350°.

Prepare squid as directed in recipe for Stuffed Squid*, above.

Sauté the onions and garlic in the oil until the onion is soft, about 2 minutes. Add the remaining ingredients, except the tomato and broth, and stir and cook 2 minutes. Chop the tomato and add to the stuffing. Fill the squid loosely about three-quarters full.

Place in a baking dish and fasten shut with a toothpick in each. Pour in the broth and bake for 20 to 25 minutes. They will swell up and look fat.

Remove the toothpicks and serve from the baking dish. Serves 6. About 235 calories each.

Baked Oysters with Parmesan Cheese

Ostriche alla Parmigiana

6 oysters on the half shell
½ teaspoon lemon juice
1 teaspoon Parmesan cheese

½ teaspoon bread crumbs
¼ teaspoon butter

Preheat oven to 500°.

Place the oysters in a flat pan, shell down. Sprinkle the lemon juice on each. Combine the Parmesan cheese and bread crumbs and add, dividing it evenly among the oysters. Add a dot of butter and bake until the oysters are plump and the crumbs light brown, about 5 minutes.

Serves 1. About 160 calories.

Poultry

ALTHOUGH WE PAY tribute to the superiority of Italian veal and baby lamb, there is no chicken like American chicken — tender, meaty, delicate, yet flavorful. Many Italian recipes for chicken were doubtless designed to make up for what the poultry itself lacked, so it may seem like gilding the lily to use their ingenuity on our prize products, but the results certainly justify it. And speaking of serendipity, chicken is appealingly low in calories and in price. All Italian chicken is called *pollo,* whether a baby broiler, a rooster, or an old hen.

In several recent comprehensive cookbooks, calorie counts are given with recipes. It is of interest to compare a few not overrich recipes in those books with ours.

Other cookbooks		*Low-Calorie Italian Cooking*
475 (approx.)	Chicken Hunter's Style	300
625	Chicken Marengo	300
475	Chicken Rosemary	340
575	Chicken Casserole	375
425	Lemon Chicken Breasts in Foil	220

Our results are obtained, for the most part, by reducing the oil and butter, not by making meager portions.

Chicken Hunter's Style I

Pollo alla Cacciatora I

1 3½-pound chicken	1 teaspoon salt
2 tablespoons olive oil	¼ teaspoon pepper
2 medium onions, sliced	a pinch sugar
1 clove garlic, crushed	1 teaspoon oregano
1 can (1 pound) peeled Italian plum tomatoes	¼ cup white wine

Cut the chicken into serving pieces and brown in the oil, turning to brown evenly. Remove and set aside. Sauté the onions and garlic in the skillet until translucent. Add the tomatoes, salt, pepper, sugar, and oregano. Stir and return the chicken to the pan. Cover and simmer for 30 minutes. Add the wine and simmer, uncovered, until the chicken is tender, about 25 minutes. Adjust the seasoning.

Serves 6. About 300 calories each.

Chicken Hunter's Style II

Pollo alla Cacciatora II

1 3½- to 4-pound frying chicken	2 cloves garlic, minced
1 teaspoon salt	1 cup peeled and chopped or canned tomatoes
½ teaspoon pepper	1 green pepper, coarsely chopped
flour	½ teaspoon rosemary
1 tablespoon oil	½ pound mushrooms, sliced
1 tablespoon butter	

Cut the chicken into 8 to 10 small pieces and sprinkle with the salt and pepper. Dust with the flour and sauté in the oil and butter for about 10 minutes, turning to brown evenly. Add the garlic and stir; add the remaining ingredients except the mushrooms. Cover and simmer until the chicken is tender, about 30 minutes. Add the mushrooms and simmer for 10 minutes.

Serves 6. About 300 calories each.

Easy Italian Chicken

Pollo alla Cacciatora Facile

1 3-pound chicken, cut into
    small pieces
salt and pepper
2 tablespoons oil
2 cloves garlic, minced

1 can (6 ounces) tomato paste
1 cup water
1 can (4 ounces) sliced
    mushrooms

Sprinkle the chicken with the salt and pepper and brown in the oil, turning to brown evenly. Add the garlic. Combine the tomato paste with the water and add to the browned chicken. Cover and simmer for 25 minutes. Add the mushrooms and their liquid and cook, uncovered, for a few minutes.

Serves 4. About 300 calories each.

Chicken Marengo I

Pollo alla Marengo I

1 3-pound frying chicken, cut
    into serving pieces
1 tablespoon butter
1 tablespoon oil
1 teaspoon salt
¼ teaspoon pepper

2 tablespoons flour
2 tablespoons water
½ cup white wine
1 tablespoon minced parsley
1 teaspoon lemon juice

Sauté the chicken in the butter and oil, sprinkle with the salt and pepper, and continue to cook until brown on all sides. Stir in the flour; add the water and then the wine while stirring. Cover and simmer for 30 minutes. Sprinkle with the parsley and lemon juice.

Serves 4. About 300 calories each.

Chicken Marengo II

Pollo alla Marengo II

1 3-pound frying chicken, cut
  into serving pieces
1 teaspoon salt
¼ teaspoon pepper
2 tablespoons oil
8 small cooked onions
1 clove garlic, crushed

¼ pound mushrooms, sliced
1 can (6 ounces) tomato paste
½ cup chicken broth
½ teaspoon oregano
flour
2 tablespoons minced parsley
  (garnish)

Season the chicken with the salt and pepper and brown in the oil, turning several times. Add onions, garlic, and mushrooms and sauté 2 minutes. Combine the tomato paste and broth and add to the chicken with the oregano. Cover and simmer for about 35 minutes. If the juices are not thick enough, thicken with a little flour and water paste and simmer for 10 minutes uncovered. Sprinkle with parsley.

  Serves 4. About 340 calories each.

Broiled Chicken

Pollo alla Griglia

1 3-pound or 2 1½-pound
  broilers
1 teaspoon salt

Low-Calorie Italian-Type
  Dressing* (optional)

Preheat broiler.

  Quarter the larger broiler or cut the small ones in half, or you may leave the birds whole and carve after broiling. Sprinkle with the salt and place skin side down on a broiler pan about 4 inches from the heat. After 15 minutes brush with the dressing, if you wish. Turn, brush again, and cook for 15 to 20 minutes more. The chicken should be an even brown.

  Serves 4. About 245 calories each.

Broiled Lemon Chicken

Pollo alla Griglia con Limone

2 1½- to 2-pound broilers, split   1 teaspoon paprika
¼ cup lemon juice   ½ teaspoon pepper
2 tablespoons broth   1 teaspoon sugar
1 tablespoon grated onion

Preheat broiler.

Place the chickens skin side down on a broiler pan. Combine the remaining ingredients. Brush on the chicken, broil for 15 minutes, baste, and turn. Baste again and broil for 20 minutes, brushing with the marinade once or twice. When the chickens are brown, serve with any remaining marinade poured over.

Serves 4. About 290 calories each.

Broiled Chicken with Oregano

Pollo Oreganato

1 3-pound frying chicken,   2 tablespoons lemon juice
   quartered   1 tablespoon minced parsley
1 teaspoon salt   1 clove garlic, minced
¼ teaspoon pepper   2 teaspoons oregano
1 tablespoon olive oil

Preheat broiler.

Sprinkle the chicken with the salt and pepper. Combine the remaining ingredients and mix thoroughly. Brush the chicken on both sides with the mixture. Place on broiler rack skin side up, brush, and broil about 4 inches from the heat for 20 minutes. Brush again with the mixture, turn, brush again, and broil for 15 minutes more. Serve with any remaining liquid poured over.

Serves 4. About 300 calories each.

Marinated Broiled Chicken

Pollo Marinato al Ferri

1 3- to 3½-pound frying
   chicken, quartered
3 tablespoons lemon juice
1 tablespoon olive oil
1 clove garlic, crushed

2 tablespoons minced parsley
1 teaspoon thyme
1 teaspoon salt
¼ teaspoon pepper

Place the chicken in a deep plate. Combine the remaining ingredients and pour over the chicken. Refrigerate in the marinade for 2 hours.

Preheat broiler.

Broil for about 20 minutes on each side, brushing frequently with the marinade.

Serves 4. About 300 calories each.

Roast Chicken

Pollo Arrosto

1 3-pound chicken
2 teaspoons salt

1 lemon (optional)
broth or water

Preheat oven to 375°.

Remove the giblets and any fat from inside the body of the bird, reserving both. Wipe the chicken and rub it inside and out with salt. Cut the lemon and squeeze some juice inside the bird and all over the skin, if you wish, and place half the lemon inside the body.

Place on a rack in a roasting pan breast side up. Put the fat from inside the body over the breast and roast, uncovered, for about 1 hour. If the chicken browns too fast, place a piece of foil loosely over the bird, tent fashion. Add ½ cup of broth or water and baste once or twice with the drippings, while the chicken is roasting.

If you want gravy, boil the neck and giblets in 2 cups of water with a few celery leaves and sprigs of parsley and

½ teaspoon salt. Strain, degrease, and add the defatted juices from the roasting pan. Thicken with a little flour and water paste.

Serves 4. About 270 calories each.

Chicken Roasted in Parchment or Foil

Pollo alla Cartoccio

1 chicken, about 3 pounds	1 teaspoon rosemary or
½ teaspoon salt	oregano
1 clove garlic, crushed	

Preheat the oven to 400°.

Brush the chicken inside and out with a mixture of the salt, garlic, and rosemary or oregano. Cut foil, parchment paper, or oiled brown paper into a large square.

Place the chicken on the foil and wrap envelope fashion, so no juice will leak out. Bake for 1 hour. Reduce the oven to 350° and cook for 30 minutes more.

Unwrap at the table to savor the chicken aroma, and pour the juices over the chicken.

Serves 4. About 250 calories each.

Baked Ginger Chicken

Pollo al Forno con Zenzero

1 3-pound chicken	2 teaspoons grated fresh or ½
3 tablespoons chicken broth	teaspoon preserved ginger
2 tablespoons sherry	1 teaspoon salt
2 tablespoons wine or wine vinegar	

Preheat oven to 350°.

Put the chicken in a bowl and pour a mixture of the remaining ingredients over. Place in the refrigerator for 12 to 15 hours, turning several times.

When ready to cook, put the chicken in a roasting pan

and bake for 1 hour, basting several times with the marinade. If the chicken is not brown enough, turn the oven to 500° for about 10 minutes, watching carefully.

Put the chicken on a warm platter. Add the remaining marinade to the pan juices and bring to a boil on top of the stove. Pour the sauce over; it should not be thick.

Serves 4. About 310 calories each.

Baked Chicken with Barbecue Sauce

Pollo con Salsa per Arrosto

2 frying chickens, about 3
  pounds each
⅓ cup wine vinegar
½ cup water
½ cup catsup or barbecue
  sauce

¼ cup Worcestershire sauce
3 teaspoons prepared mustard
¼ cup chopped onion
1 clove garlic, crushed

Preheat oven to 375°.

Cut the chicken into quarters or smaller pieces. Combine the remaining ingredients and simmer for 15 minutes.

Place the chicken in a shallow baking pan, pour half the sauce over, and bake for 25 minutes. Turn the chicken, bake for 25 minutes more, basting with the sauce several times. Pour any remaining sauce over and cook for 10 minutes more.

Serves 8. About 300 calories each.

Spicy Chicken

Pollo Piccante

1 chicken, about 3 pounds, cut
  into serving pieces
2 tablespoons vegetable oil
1 teaspoon Worcestershire
  sauce

½ teaspoon Tabasco sauce
½ teaspoon pepper
½ teaspoon paprika
pinch red pepper
2 to 3 tablespoons lemon juice

Preheat oven to 375°.

Place the chicken in a bowl. Combine the remaining ingredients and pour over the chicken. Let stand for 2 or 3 hours, turning several times.

Place the chicken in a baking pan and bake for 1 hour, basting frequently with the marinade. Just before serving, pour the marinade over the chicken, heat, and serve.

Serves 4. About 300 calories each.

Rosemary Chicken

Pollo con Rosmarino

1 3-pound fryer, cut into serving pieces	1 tablespoon minced onion
flour	½ cup water
1 teaspoon salt	½ cup white wine
¼ teaspoon pepper	1 tablespoon fresh or 2 teaspoons dried rosemary
2 tablespoons butter	

Shake the chicken pieces in a bag with the flour mixed with the salt and pepper. Brown in the butter, adding the onion. When evenly brown, add the water, wine, and rosemary. Cover and simmer for 30 minutes. Uncover and cook for a few minutes.

Serves 4. About 340 calories each.

Chicken with Mushrooms

Pollo ai Funghi

Proceed as for Rosemary Chicken*. Sauté ½ pound sliced mushrooms for 2 minutes in 2 tablespoons butter and add to the chicken for the last few minutes of the covered cooking.

Serves 4. About 395 calories each.

Chicken in a Casserole

Pollo in Casseruola

1 3-pound chicken
1 teaspoon salt
1 medium onion, sliced thin
1 tablespoon olive oil
1 tablespoon butter
1 stalk celery, chopped fine

½ cup white wine
1 can (8 ounces) tomato
   purée
1 pound mushrooms, sliced
2 tablespoons minced parsley

Cut the chicken into serving pieces and sprinkle with the salt. Sauté the onion in the oil and butter for a minute in a casserole; add the chicken and brown on all sides. Add the celery, wine, and tomato purée.

Cover and simmer for 25 minutes, turning the chicken a few times. Add the mushrooms and cook for 10 minutes more. Add the parsley and adjust the seasoning. Serve in the casserole.

Serves 4. About 375 calories each.

Chicken Divan Florentine

Pollo alla Fiorentina

2 packages frozen chopped
   spinach
2 tablespoons butter
2 tablespoons flour

1 cup skim milk
3 tablespoons grated
   Parmesan cheese
sliced cooked chicken

Preheat oven to 400°.

Cook the spinach in 2 tablespoons water for 2 minutes. Melt the butter (do not brown); blend in the flour and pour in the milk slowly while stirring. Stir in half the cheese. Cook and stir until slightly thickened.

Put the spinach into a baking dish, pour over half the sauce, spread the chicken slices over the sauce and pour over the remaining sauce. Top with the remaining cheese and bake for about 15 minutes until the cheese is slightly brown and the casserole bubbly.

Serves 4. About 395 calories each.

Chicken with Egg Sauce

Pollo in Salsa d'Uovo

1 3-pound chicken, quartered
2 tablespoons butter
1 teaspoon salt
¼ teaspoon pepper

1 tablespoon flour
1 cup chicken broth
1 teaspoon lemon juice
1 egg yolk

Brown the chicken in the butter, turning to brown evenly. Sprinkle with the salt and pepper and the flour and stir to brown. Pour in the broth; cover and simmer for 40 minutes. Remove the chicken to a hot platter and keep warm.

Beat the lemon juice and egg yolk and pour into the juices in the pan. Heat and stir until smooth and thickened; do not boil. Pour over the chicken.

Serves 4. About 360 calories each.

Chicken with Mushrooms in Tomato Sauce

Pollo alla Salsa di Pomidoro con Funghi

1 3-pound frying chicken, cut into serving pieces
1½ tablespoons vegetable or olive oil
3 tablespoons minced onion
1 tablespoon butter

2 tablespoons chicken broth
½ pound mushrooms
¼ cup tomato sauce
1 teaspoon lemon juice
½ teaspoon oregano and/or basil

Sauté the chicken in oil over medium heat, turning to brown evenly. Continue to cook slowly for about 30 minutes.

Meanwhile, sauté the onion in the butter for 2 minutes. Add the broth and the mushrooms, whole if they are small, cut in half if large. Sauté for 3 minutes while stirring. Add the tomato sauce, lemon juice, and herb. Simmer for 2 or 3 minutes.

Serve the chicken on a warm platter with the sauce poured over.

Serves 4. About 360 calories each.

Chicken with Tomatoes and Vermouth

Pollo al Pomidoro e Vermut

1 3½-pound chicken, cut into
  serving pieces
1 can (1 pound) peeled Italian
  plum tomatoes

1 bay leaf
pinch oregano
½ cup dry vermouth

Simmer the chicken with the tomatoes, bay leaf, and oregano for 30 minutes. Add the vermouth; cover and simmer for 15 minutes more until the chicken is tender.
Serves 4. About 340 calories each.

Deviled Chicken

Pollo alla Diavola

1 3-pound chicken
1 teaspoon salt
½ teaspoon cayenne pepper
¼ teaspoon pepper

1 clove garlic, crushed
1 teaspoon lemon juice
1 tablespoon oil
few drops Tabasco sauce

Place the chicken skin side down on a board and cut down the backbone, not cutting all the way through. Turn, push flat, and beat with a mallet, rolling pin, or bottle so it stays flat.
Combine the remaining ingredients and pour over the chicken. Let stand an hour.
Preheat broiler if cooking indoors.
Grill the chicken about 5 inches from the heat indoors or out. Turn after 15 minutes and broil the other side. Brush several times with the marinade and continue to cook a little farther from the heat for another 20 minutes.
Serves 4. About 315 calories each.

Lemon Chicken Breasts in Foil

Petti di Pollo al Limone

3 chicken breasts, skinned
  and boned
1 tablespoon minced fresh or 2
  teaspoons dried tarragon

2 tablespoons minced chives
  or scallions
juice of 3 lemons
1 teaspoon salt

Preheat oven to 375°.

Split the chicken breasts in half and place each on a square of foil. Sprinkle with the tarragon, put part of the chives or scallions on each, and sprinkle with the lemon juice and the salt.

Close the foil envelope fashion, making sure no juice can leak out. Bake for 30 minutes.

Serve in the foil so each person will savor the fragrance.

Serves 6. About 220 calories each.

Sautéed Chicken Breasts

Petti di Pollo Sautè

2 chicken breasts, about 1⅓
  pounds, sliced very thin
1 teaspoon salt
¼ teaspoon pepper
2 eggs, beaten

¼ cup bread crumbs
2 tablespoons oil
1 tablespoon butter
1 tablespoon lemon juice

Pound the sliced chicken breasts to make them thin. Combine the salt and pepper with the eggs. Dip the chicken in the seasoned eggs and dust with the crumbs.

Sauté in a mixture of the oil and butter in a large skillet, turning once after about 8 minutes. The total cooking time should be no more than 15 minutes. Sprinkle with the lemon juice.

Serves 4. About 325 calories each.

Chicken Breasts with White Grapes

Petti di Pollo con Uvo Bianco

3 whole chicken breasts,
   skinned, boned, and split
½ teaspoon salt
¼ teaspoon pepper

2 tablespoons vegetable oil
½ cup white wine
1 pound seedless white grapes
2 tablespoons flour

Preheat oven to 375°.

Place the breasts in a low baking dish. They must lie flat. Sprinkle with the salt, pepper, and oil. Pour the wine over and add the grapes. Cover and bake for 40 minutes.

Remove the chicken to a warm platter. Add a paste of the flour and water to the drippings. Stir and cook until smooth and thickened. Adjust the seasoning and pour over the chicken.

Serves 6. About 235 calories each.

Chicken Breasts in Tomato Sauce

Petti di Pollo al Pomidoro

3 large chicken breasts, 2 to
   2½ pounds, boned and split
1 teaspoon salt
¼ teaspoon pepper
1 teaspoon oregano or
   tarragon

1 clove garlic, crushed
1 medium onion, sliced thin
1 can (1 pound) Italian
   tomatoes
½ pound mushrooms, sliced
2 tablespoons minced parsley

Preheat oven to 375°.

Sprinkle the chicken with the salt, pepper, herb, and garlic. Place in a baking dish, add the onion, and pour the tomatoes over. Bake, covered, for 30 minutes. Add a little water or tomato juice if it is too dry. Add the mushrooms and parsley and bake for 20 minutes more. Serve from the baking dish or on a platter with all juices poured over.

Serves 6. About 200 calories each.

Golden Turkey Fillets

Petto di Tacchino Dorado

6 slices turkey breast, about 2
   pounds
flour
1 teaspoon salt
2 eggs, beaten

2 tablespoons butter
1 tablespoon oil
1 tablespoon lemon juice or
   lemon wedges

Pound the meat thin, removing any skin. Dust with the flour, sprinkle with the salt, and dip in the beaten egg.

Sauté in the butter and oil until golden brown, turning once. The total cooking time should not exceed 15 minutes. Sprinkle with lemon juice or serve with lemon wedges.

Serves 6. About 310 calories each.

Turkey Breast with Wine Sauce

Filetti di Tacchino al Vino

6 slices turkey breast, about 2
   pounds
flour
1 teaspoon salt
¼ teaspoon pepper

2 tablespoons butter
1 tablespoon oil
½ cup sherry or white wine
¼ teaspoon sugar if using
   white wine

Pound the turkey slices to make them quite thin. Dust very lightly with the flour and sprinkle with the salt and pepper. Make incisions around the edges so they will lie flat.

Sauté in the butter and oil, browning on both sides. The total cooking time should be about 15 minutes. Remove to a warm platter and keep hot.

Add the wine (and sugar, if necessary) to the pan, scraping up any brown bits, and boil and stir for 2 minutes. Pour over the turkey fillets.

Serves 6. About 280 calories each.

Cooked Turkey Breast with Tomatoes

Petto di Tacchino al Pomidoro

6 slices cooked turkey breast,
  about 2 pounds
2 tablespoons butter
4 tomatoes, peeled and
  chopped, or 1 can (14
  ounces) Italian tomatoes

½ teaspoon salt
¼ teaspoon sugar
1 teaspoon basil
2 tablespoons minced parsley
  (garnish)

Preheat oven to 350°.

Put the turkey slices into the bottom of a large buttered casserole or baking dish. Cover with the tomatoes and sprinkle with the salt, sugar, and basil. Bake for 20 minutes. Top with parsley and serve from the dish.

Serves 6. About 235 calories each.

Roast Pheasant

Fagiano al Forno

1 hen pheasant, 3 pounds
salt and pepper

2 slices bacon
½ cup chicken broth
1 tablespoon minced parsley

Preheat oven to 450°.

Wipe the pheasant dry, season with the salt and pepper, and tie the legs close to the body. Put 1 strip of bacon over the breast and the other, cut in half, over the legs. Roast for 30 minutes, reduce the heat to 350°, and bake for 30 minutes more, until tender. Baste with a little chicken broth several times. Do not baste with the drippings, which will be mostly bacon fat.

Remove the bird to a platter and keep warm. Remove as much fat as you can from the drippings. Add the remaining broth and stir and loosen any brown bits from the pan. Boil for 1 or 2 minutes and strain. Add parsley and pour over the pheasant.

Serves 4. About 415 calories each.

Broiled Pheasant

Fagiano alla Griglia

1 large pheasant, about 3   ¼ teaspoon pepper
  pounds   1 clove garlic, crushed
1 teaspoon salt   2 tablespoons melted butter

Preheat broiler.

Split the pheasant in half and sprinkle with the salt and pepper. Add the garlic to the butter and brush the bird with it.

Put on a broiler rack skin side down. Broil about 5 inches from the heat for 20 minutes. Turn, brush with the butter, and broil another 15 minutes until brown.

Serves 4. About 400 calories each.

Rabbit Stew

Coniglio in Umido

1 4-pound rabbit, cut into   2 stalks celery, sliced
  serving pieces   3 tomatoes, peeled and
1 tablespoon oil   chopped
1 tablespoon butter   1 cup white wine
1 clove garlic, crushed   ½ to 1 teaspoon salt
1 large onion, sliced   ¼ teaspoon pepper
½ teaspoon thyme or rosemary   ¼ teaspoon nutmeg
1 carrot, sliced thin   flour

Sauté the rabbit in the oil and butter in a casserole, turning to brown evenly. Add the garlic, onion, and thyme, and stir for 2 or 3 minutes. Add the carrot, celery, tomatoes, and wine. Cover and simmer for 1 hour.

Add the salt, pepper, and nutmeg for the last half-hour of cooking. The amount of salt will depend upon the seasoning in the broth.

Serve from the casserole or put into a warm serving bowl. Thicken the juices slightly with a little flour and water paste.

Serves 6. About 375 calories each.

Roast Rabbit

Coniglio al Forno

1 large rabbit, about 4 pounds
1 tablespoon vinegar
1 tablespoon water
1 teaspoon salt
¼ teaspoon pepper

½ teaspoon rosemary
2 tablespoons oil
1 medium onion, sliced thin
½ cup broth or white wine or
  water

Preheat oven to 450°.

Wipe the rabbit with the vinegar and water combined. Sprinkle with the salt, pepper, and rosemary. Brush with the oil and put any remaining oil in the roaster with the rabbit and onion.

Roast for 20 minutes until the rabbit is browned. Reduce the heat to 350°, add the broth, and roast, covered, for another 30 minutes, or until tender (it depends upon the age of the rabbit). Baste from time to time. Serve with the onion and any juice poured over.

Serves 6. About 350 calories each.

Sweet and Sour Rabbit

Coniglio Dolce e Agro

1 slice salt pork, about 1 by 2
  inches, diced
1 3- to 4-pound rabbit, cut into
  serving pieces
2 onions, chopped

1 can (8 ounces) tomato paste
¼ cup wine vinegar
2 teaspoons sugar
1 tablespoon minced parsley

Sauté the salt pork until crisp. Remove and set aside to drain on paper toweling.

Sauté the rabbit and onions in the pork drippings. Brown evenly and add the tomato paste, vinegar, and sugar. Cover tight and simmer until tender, about 30 minutes.

Add the parsley, salt, and more sugar to taste.

Serves 4 to 6. About 460 to 320 calories each.

Meat

ALL MEAT is high in calories, but it is also high in vitamins and other valuable components. For a well-balanced diet, do not cut down too much on meat. Do cut off all visible fat! Italians have a slight preference for the white-fleshed meats, veal and pork. Americans are beef eaters. Actually, all meats have about the same calorie count, so choose the ones you prefer. Lean beef round has 617 calories per pound; lean leg of lamb, 595; lean pork leg, 694; and veal, 740. A pound of meat usually makes three servings.

In each of the four meat sections, the very new, exciting concept of not overcooking, cooking with herbs, various seasonings, and broth instead of fat keeps the Italian meat flavor up and the calories down. There is something in the saying "Meat makes the meal." With this new attitude toward Italian cooking, you will be able to serve meat without feeling guilty.

BEEF

In Italy beef, *manzo*, is usually served in small pieces, such as steak (*bistecca*, named after our beef steak) and fillets. They are much more popular than a standing rib roast. Small pieces come to the table in stews and ragouts and also on skewers. Still smaller pieces arrive as meatballs and in pasta sauces. You won't be disappointed in these new slim-lined recipes.

Broiled Steak

Bistecca

1 sirloin or porterhouse steak,
  3 to 3½ pounds

1 teaspoon salt
½ teaspoon pepper

Preheat broiler.

Cut all visible fat from the steak. Broil it close to the heat for 4 minutes, sprinkle with half the salt and pepper, and turn it. Broil for 3 minutes more and sprinkle with the remaining salt and pepper. You need no butter or oil.

If you wish a better-done steak, cook it 1 minute longer on each side. Also, it is better grilled over charcoal than under the broiler.

Serves 6. About 315 calories each.

Florentine Steak

Bistecca alla Fiorentina

1 3- to 3½-pound porterhouse
  or sirloin steak
1 teaspoon olive oil

2 teaspoons lemon juice
1 teaspoon salt
½ teaspoon pepper

Preheat broiler if cooking indoors.

Rub the steak lightly with the oil. Broil over charcoal or in the broiler for 3 or 4 minutes on each side, depending on the thickness of the steak. It should be served rare or medium, not well done.

Sprinkle with the lemon juice and salt and pepper before you turn it and again after.

Serves 4 to 6. About 450 calories each for 4; about 325 calories each for 6.

Steak on a Skewer

Spiedini di Bistecca

2 pounds lean beef steaks,
    sirloin or fillet
2 tablespoons beef broth
2 tablespoons red wine
1 clove garlic, crushed

½ teaspoon salt
¼ teaspoon pepper
¼ teaspoon sugar
3 not too ripe large tomatoes,
    cut in eighths

Cut the steak into ½-inch cubes. Combine the remaining ingredients except the tomatoes and marinate the steak for 3 or 4 hours in the mixture.

Preheat broiler if cooking indoors.

String on 6 long skewers, putting each tomato wedge after 2 or 3 steak cubes.

Broil for 3 minutes close to the heat, brush with the marinade, turn, brush again, and broil for 2 minutes more. Brush with the marinade again before serving.

Serves 6. About 250 calories each.

Broiled Fillets of Beef

Filetti di Manzo alla Griglia

1⅓ pounds fillet of beef, cut
    into 4 pieces
1 clove garlic, halved (optional)

1 tablespoon olive oil
½ teaspoon salt
¼ teaspoon pepper

Preheat broiler if cooking indoors.

Have the meat at room temperature and trim off the fat. Rub each piece with the cut clove of garlic, if you wish. Brush with the oil on both sides.

Broil on a heated grill close to the source of the heat, turning once. To insure the degree of doneness you want, cut a tiny slit in the edge. If it is too rare, move the meat farther away from the heat for a minute or two. Sprinkle with salt and pepper.

Serves 4. About 235 calories each.

Pan-Fried Fillet of Beef

Filetti di Manzo in Padella

1⅓ pounds fillet of beef   1 cup coarse salt

Have the fillets cut as for Broiled Fillet of Beef*. Salt an iron skillet heavily and heat it without burning. This may be done carefully on top of the stove or in a very hot oven. Put the fillets on top of the salt, cook for 2 minutes, and turn to cook the other side.

Serves 4. About 135 calories each.

Roast Beef with Mushrooms

Manzo ai Funghi

1 piece lean eye round or eye rib of beef, about 2 pounds
3 tablespoons oil
1 teaspoon salt
¼ teaspoon pepper

1 large onion or 2 shallots, sliced
¾ pound mushrooms, sliced
½ cup sherry, Madeira, or red wine

Preheat oven to 375°.

Trim any fat from the meat. Brush it with half the oil. Brown it on both sides in a large iron skillet or a shallow baking pan. Sprinkle with the salt and pepper and bake for 30 to 40 minutes. Test for doneness by making a small slit with a small pointed knife. The beef should be rare.

Meanwhile, sauté the onions or shallots in the remaining oil for 2 minutes until transparent. Add the mushrooms; stir and cook for 2 minutes more. Add the wine; cover and cook for 1 minute.

Carve the beef and pass the very hot mushroom sauce.

Serves 6. About 300 calories each.

Beef Stew

Umido di Carne

2 pounds lean beef cut into 1-
   to 1½-inch cubes
2 tablespoons oil or butter
2 onions, chopped
2 cloves garlic, minced

½ cup broth
½ cup red wine
¼ teaspoon pepper
1 can (14 ounces) Italian
   tomatoes

Sauté the meat in the oil or butter in a heavy pot, turning frequently to brown evenly. Be careful not to burn. Add the onions and garlic and cook and stir until brown. Add the remaining ingredients, cover, and simmer until the beef is tender, about 40 minutes.

Serves 6. About 300 calories each.

Beef Ragout

Ragù di Manzo

2 pounds lean beef, cut into 1-
   inch cubes
3 cups beef broth
1 clove garlic, cut
½ teaspoon pepper
½ teaspoon oregano or thyme

2 cups sliced carrots
2 cups sliced celery
½ pound mushroooms
1 pound small white onions
flour (optional)

Preheat broiler.

Place the beef on a cookie sheet and brown under the broiler, turning to brown evenly. Put into a pot with the broth, garlic, pepper, and oregano or thyme. Cover and simmer for 1 to 1½ hours until the meat is almost tender.

Add the carrots and celery and cook for 20 minutes. Add the mushrooms and onions and cook for 15 minutes more.

Remove the garlic, taste for seasoning, and thicken, if you wish, with a little flour and water paste.

Serves 8. About 230 calories each.

Three-Meat Stew

Ragù

1 large onion, minced
2 tablespoons butter or oil
1 pound lean beef, cut into 1-inch cubes
½ pound lean pork, cut into 1-inch cubes
½ pound veal, cut into 1-inch cubes
2 cups water or part broth, part water

½ teaspoon paprika
1 teaspoon salt
¼ teaspoon pepper
1 can (8 ounces) Italian peeled tomatoes
flour (optional)
1 cup sour cream (optional)

Sauté the onion in the butter until light brown. Remove and drain on paper toweling. In a large pan brown the pork; add the veal and brown; add the beef and brown.

Return the onions to the pan and add the water or broth, paprika, salt, and pepper. Cover and simmer for 1 hour; add the tomatoes and simmer for 30 minutes, until the beef is tender.

If you want a thicker sauce, thicken with a little flour and water paste or sour cream stirred in just before serving. Heat but do not boil.

Serves 6. About 300 calories each without sour cream.

Meatballs

Polpette

2 pounds ground lean beef
½ teaspoon salt
¼ teaspoon pepper
½ teaspoon oregano

½ teaspoon garlic salt or 1 clove garlic, crushed
1 egg, beaten
¼ cup strong beef broth

Combine the beef with remaining ingredients, using only 2 tablespoons of the beef broth. Form into balls. Bring the remaining broth to a boil in a skillet. Add the balls and cook for 10 minutes, turning to cook evenly.

Serves 4. About 300 calories each.

Meatballs in Tomato Sauce

Polpette al Sugo di Pomidoro

2 slices white bread
1 pound ground lean beef
1 clove garlic, minced
1 teaspoon salt
¼ teaspoon pepper
⅛ teaspoon nutmeg

2 eggs, beaten
¼ cup chopped parsley
Basic Tomato Sauce* or 1 can (14 ounces) tomato sauce

Soak the bread for 3 minutes in water to cover. Squeeze out the moisture and put it into a bowl with the remaining ingredients except the tomato sauce. Mix thoroughly with the hands. Form into balls about 1 to 1½ inches in diameter.

Heat the tomato sauce and drop balls into it gently and simmer for 12 to 15 minutes.

Serves 4. About 290 calories each.

Meatballs with Wine

Polpettine con Vino

2 slices white bread
1 pound ground lean beef
1 teaspoon salt
¼ teaspoon pepper
pinch nutmeg

¼ teaspoon oregano
flour
2 tablespoons oil
½ cup red or white wine

Soak the bread for a few minutes in a little warm water to cover and squeeze dry. Put into a bowl with the beef and the seasonings and mix thoroughly with the hands.

Form into balls about 1 inch in diameter. Roll lightly in the flour and sauté in the oil until browned on all sides, 2 or 3 minutes. Add the wine; cover and cook for 10 minutes. Serve with any juices poured over.

Serves 4. About 325 calories each.

Meatballs with Marsala

Polpette di Manzo al Marsala

1 pound ground lean beef
1 teaspoon salt
¼ teaspoon pepper
½ teaspoon sage
2 tablespoons grated
  Parmesan cheese

flour
2 tablespoons butter
¼ cup Marsala

Combine the beef, salt, pepper, sage, and cheese. Mix thoroughly with the hands. Form into small balls and roll lightly in the flour. Brown in the butter, turning to brown evenly, for 3 or 4 minutes. Add the Marsala and let it come to a boil and reduce. Serve the meatballs with the juice poured over.

Serves 4. About 325 calories each.

Beef-Eggplant Casserole

Manzo con Melanzane in Umido

1 1-pound eggplant
juice of 1 lemon
1½ pounds ground lean beef
¼ cup seasoned bread crumbs

1 teaspoon oregano
1 teaspoon salt
¼ teaspoon pepper
1 tablespoon grated cheese

Preheat oven to 350°.

Peel the eggplant and cut it into slices about ⅓ inch thick. Sprinkle the slices with the lemon juice. Combine the beef, bread crumbs, oregano, salt, and pepper.

Put a layer of eggplant slices into a casserole, cover with one third of the meat mixture and repeat two more times. Top with the cheese and bake for about 1 hour.

Serves 6. About 200 calories each.

VEAL

Italy is famous for its many dishes featuring veal, *vitello,* a milk-fed calf. If you know an Italian butcher, you will probably be able to buy baby veal. If not, you can make do with any veal. You may pound it with a mallet, rolling pin, or a bottle to make thin and tender *scaloppine.* This is the most popular cut of veal in Italy. There it is frequently doused with olive oil and sauces that can be cut to a minimum and still provide superb eating.

Thin Veal Cutlets

Scaloppine

1⅓ pounds veal cutlets, cut
   very thin
2 tablespoons flour
½ teaspoon salt

¼ teaspoon pepper
3 tablespoons butter
¼ cup white wine

Pound the veal flat and dust with a mixture of the flour, salt, and pepper. Brown in the butter for 3 minutes on each side. Add the wine, cover, and cook for 2 minutes. Serves 4. About 315 calories each.

Veal Scallopine with Lemon

Piccate di Vitello al Limone

1½ pounds thin veal cutlets
1 teaspoon salt
¼ teaspoon pepper
flour

2 tablespoons oil or butter or a
   combination of the two
2 tablespoons lemon juice
lemon slices

Pound the veal thin, sprinkle with the salt and pepper, and dust thoroughly with the flour. Brown in the oil or butter, turning once to brown the other side. Add the lemon juice and simmer for 4 minutes. Serve with lemon slices.

Serves 4. About 315 calories each.

Veal Scallopine with Wine

Scaloppine di Vitello al Vino

1½ pounds veal cutlets, cut
  thin
½ teaspoon salt
¼ teaspoon pepper
1 beef bouillon cube
3 tablespoons water

½ clove garlic, cut
¼ cup wine: red, white, or
  sherry
3 tablespoons tomato sauce
2 tablespoons minced parsley

Pound the veal flat. Sprinkle with the salt and pepper. Dissolve the bouillon cube in the water with the garlic. Put into a skillet, bring to a boil, and brown the veal in it on both sides. Add the wine, tomato sauce, and parsley and bring to a boil to evaporate the alcohol.

Place the veal on a serving plate. Remove the garlic. Pour the sauce over.

Serves 4. About 265 calories each.

Rolls of Veal and Ham

Saltimbocca alla Romana

1 pound veal cutlets, cut thin
½ teaspoon salt
½ teaspoon or 8 small leaves
  sage
¼ pound lean prosciutto or
  other ham, sliced very thin

flour
2 tablespoons butter
⅓ cup white wine

Pound the veal thin and cut into 8 pieces. Sprinkle with the salt and sage. Trim the fat from the ham, cut it into 8 pieces, and place it over the veal. Roll and fasten with toothpicks.

Dust with the flour and brown in the butter until golden on all sides. Place on a hot platter and remove the toothpicks.

Pour the wine into the pan and stir with a wooden spoon to loosen any brown bits. Bring to a boil and pour over the veal rolls.

Serves 4. About 280 calories each.

Herbed Veal Chops

Costolette di Vitello con Erbe

6 veal chops, trimmed
2 tablespoons oil or butter or a
   combination of the two
1 teaspoon salt
¼ teaspoon pepper

2 tablespoons minced parsley
½ teaspoon basil
½ teaspoon sage
⅓ cup chicken broth

Sauté the veal chops in oil or butter over high heat, turning to brown evenly. Sprinkle with the remaining ingredients except the broth and continue to cook over low heat for 10 minutes, turning several times. Add the broth and cook for 10 minutes more.

Remove the chops to a heated platter. Adjust the seasoning of the liquid. Stir, bring to a boil, and pour over the chops.

Serves 6. About 250 calories each.

Veal Chops with Green Beans

Costolette di Vitello con Fagiolini

6 lean veal chops
1 teaspoon sugar
2 medium onions, sliced thin
1 teaspoon salt
¼ teaspoon pepper
½ teaspoon oregano

1 cup chicken broth
1 jar (4 ounces) pimientos,
   cut up
1 package (10 ounces) frozen
   cut green beans, thawed

Sprinkle the chops with the sugar and brown in a very hot skillet, turning once. Add the onions and seasonings and stir in the broth. Cover and simmer for 25 minutes. Add the pimientos and beans and simmer for 10 to 12 minutes.

Serves 6. About 285 calories each.

Veal Chops with Peppers

Costolette di Vitello con Peperoni

6 veal chops, trimmed
3 tablespoons olive oil
3 onions, sliced thin
3 peppers, green or red, cut into thin strips

2 cups peeled fresh or canned tomatoes
1 teaspoon salt
¼ teaspoon pepper

Sauté the chops in 1 tablespoon of the oil, turning to brown evenly. Sauté the onions and peppers in the remaining oil in a separate pan until the onions are transparent and light brown. Add to the chops with the tomatoes, salt, and pepper, and stir and cook for 10 minutes.

Serves 6. About 300 calories each.

Veal Chops with Mushrooms

Costolette di Vitello ai Funghi

6 loin veal chops
1 teaspoon salt
¼ teaspoon pepper
flour
1 tablespoon olive oil
2 medium onions, sliced

½ pound mushrooms, quartered
1 green pepper, chopped, or 1 jar (4 ounces) pimientos, chopped
1 cup chicken broth

Sprinkle the chops with the salt and pepper and dust with the flour. Sauté in very hot oil, turning to brown evenly, for 3 minutes on each side.

Add the onions and sauté until lightly browned. Add

the mushrooms and pepper or pimientos and cook for 2 minutes. Add the broth and cover and simmer until the chops are tender, about 15 minutes.

Serve the chops with the onion-mushroom mixture and the liquid poured over.

Serves 6. About 300 calories each.

Sautéed Veal Chops or Scallops with Lemon
Costolette di Vitello con Limone

1½ pounds veal scallops or 6 chops	2 tablespoons butter
	1 tablespoon olive oil
2 tablespoons flour	3 tablespoons lemon juice
1 teaspoon salt	2 tablespoons minced parsley
½ teaspoon pepper	

Dust the scallops or chops with the flour mixed with the salt and pepper. Sauté in a mixture of the butter and oil, turning to brown evenly. Scallops take about 5 minutes, chops about 15 minutes, total cooking time.

Remove to a platter. Add the lemon juice and parsley to the pan, heat, and pour over the veal.

Serves 6. About 285 calories each.

Veal Pot Roast
Fetta di Vitello

2½-pound boneless veal roast, preferably rump	1 teaspoon salt
	¼ teaspoon pepper
2 tablespoons butter	¼ tablespoon sugar
1 medium onion, chopped	1 pound carrots, scraped and
1 clove garlic, minced	cut into thin strips
½ cup broth	1 or 2 tablespoons flour

Preheat oven to 350° if used.

Brown the veal on all sides in the butter. Add the onion and garlic and brown. Pour in the broth and add the salt, pepper, and sugar. Cover and simmer for 30 minutes or bake for 45 minutes. Add the carrots and cook for about 20 minutes, until the meat is tender.

Skim off all the fat and serve with the juices thickened with the flour.

Serves 6. About 310 calories each.

Veal Stew with White Wine
Stufatino

2 slices bacon or salt pork	½ cup tomato sauce
1 large onion, chopped	1 cup white wine
1 large clove garlic, minced	1 teaspoon salt
2 pounds lean veal, sliced	¼ teaspoon pepper
1 cup water	flour

Sauté the bacon or salt pork until crisp. Remove and set aside. Brown the onion and garlic in the drippings for 2 minutes. Add the veal and turn to brown evenly. Add the remaining ingredients except the flour; cover and simmer until the veal is tender, about 45 minutes. Add more wine or water if needed.

Thicken the juices with a little flour and water paste and adjust the seasoning.

Serves 6. About 260 calories each.

Veal Fricassee
Fricassea di Vitello

4 tablespoons butter	1 tablespoon chopped parsley
3 tablespoons flour	2 pounds lean veal, cut into 1-inch cubes
2 cups broth	
1 carrot, diced	1 teaspoon salt
1 clove garlic, minced	¼ teaspoon pepper
3 scallions, chopped	½ pound mushrooms, sliced
2 stalks celery, chopped	½ teaspoon oregano

Melt 2 tablespoons of the butter in a baking dish or casserole and blend in the flour. Pour in the broth slowly while stirring and add the vegetables, meat, salt, and pepper. Cover tight and simmer until tender, about 1 hour. Stir several times and add more broth or water if needed.

Sauté the mushrooms in the remaining 2 tablespoons of butter for 2 minutes; add the oregano and stir into the fricassee.

Serves 6. About 300 calories each.

Veal Knuckle

Osso Buco

2 or 3 veal shanks, about 4
   pounds, cut into 2-inch
   pieces
2 tablespoons flour
2 tablespoons butter
2 tablespoons olive oil
2 cloves garlic, minced
½ cup chopped carrots
½ cup chopped celery
1 cup peeled chopped
   tomatoes

½ cup beef broth
½ cup white wine
1 teaspoon salt
¼ teaspoon pepper
½ teaspoon thyme
1 bay leaf
2 teaspoons grated lemon rind
1 tablespoon minced parsley

Trim any excess fat from the veal and turn it in the flour. Brown thoroughly in a mixture of the butter and oil. Add the garlic, carrots, and celery and brown for 10 minutes. Add the tomatoes, broth, wine, and seasonings. Cover and simmer until the meat is very tender, at least 1½ hours. Remove the bay leaf. Add the lemon rind and parsley and heat for 5 minutes.

Serves 6. About 375 calories each.

Cold Veal with Tuna Sauce

Vitello Tonnato

	Sauce:
2 pounds boneless veal rump or rolled lean shoulder	2 cans (7 ounces each) tuna packed in water
1 onion, chopped	2 tablespoons lemon juice
1 carrot, chopped	2 hard-cooked eggs, chopped
3 sprigs parsley	6 anchovy fillets, cut up
1 teaspoon salt	2 tablespoons capers (garnish)

Place the veal in a deep pot with water to cover, adding the onion, carrot, parsley, and salt. Cook until tender, about 1 to 1¼ hours. Cool, wrap in foil, and refrigerate until thoroughly chilled, preferably overnight.

Sauce: Break up the tuna, add the lemon juice, eggs, and anchovies, and purée in a blender or food processor until smooth. Chill.

To serve, slice the veal thin and place it in rows on a chilled platter. Pour the tuna sauce over and garnish with capers.

Serves 4. About 395 calories each.

LAMB

Baby lamb, and also very young lamb, is known as *ab-bacchio*. A suckling lamb is hard to come by in this country except on farms or in special markets during the spring. In Italy it is often cooked on a spit and is always delicious. *Agnello* is a little older and is what we usually buy. Still older lamb is known as *moutone*, mutton. Mutton is used in stews or as chops, which are excellent. Italians are apt to use olive oil when cooking lamb; we prefer it as lean as possible, even without considering calories. If you use a marinade with oil, wipe the meat with a damp cloth before cooking.

Roast Leg of Lamb

Agnello al Forno

leg of young lamb, about 6
  pounds
2 cloves garlic, slivered, or 1
  tablespoon rosemary
  (optional)

2 teaspoons salt
½ teaspoon pepper

Preheat oven to 375°.

Wipe the lamb, trim off all visible fat, and make small slits in a number of places with a sharp knife. Insert the garlic slivers and rub with the salt and pepper. If you don't want to use the garlic, rub with the rosemary, salt, and pepper. Roast for about 1¼ hours for rare lamb, 1½ for pink, and up to 2 hours for well done. Do not cover.

Serves 8. About 325 calories each.

Roast Baby Lamb

Abbacchio al Forno

1 forequarter or leg of baby
  lamb, about 4 pounds
1 teaspoon rosemary, savory,
  thyme, or basil

1 teaspoon salt
¼ teaspoon pepper

Preheat oven to 350°.

Rub the lamb with the herb of your choice and the salt and pepper. Roast for about 1½ hours. Baby lamb should not be served rare like mature lamb.

Serves 6. About 385 calories each.

Broiled Baby Lamb Chops

Costolette d'Abbacchio alla Griglia

These chops will be very small, so some people will want more than two.

12 to 15 lamb chops
1 teaspoon salt

¼ teaspoon pepper
2 teaspoons rosemary

Preheat broiler.

Sprinkle the chops on both sides with a mixture of the salt, pepper, and rosemary, rubbing the mixture into the small, delicate chops. Grill 3 inches from the heat until brown; turn and brown the other side. They will take only about 3 minutes to a side.

Serves 6. About 200 calories each.

Lamb with Mushrooms

Agnello con Funghi

6 to 12 slices cooked lean
   lamb, depending upon size
½ cup broth
½ pound mushrooms, cut up if
   large
3 tablespoons butter
2 tablespoons flour

1 teaspoon salt
½ teaspoon pepper
2 tablespoons minced parsley
½ teaspoon dried or 1
   teaspoon chopped fresh
   mint

Moisten the lamb with ¼ cup of the broth. Sauté the mushrooms in 1 tablespoon of the butter. Dust the lamb lightly with the flour and salt and add to the mushrooms.

In a separate pan, melt the remaining 2 tablespoons of butter, blend in the remaining flour, stir in the remaining ¼ cup of broth, the parsley, and mint. Simmer until thickened. Pour over the lamb and reheat.

Serves 6. About 240 calories each.

Lamb Rollettes

Braciuoline d'Agnello

2 pounds lamb steak, sliced ¼
   inch thick
1 teaspoon salt
¼ teaspoon pepper
¼ teaspoon rosemary

2 onions, sliced
2 cloves garlic, minced
2 tablespoons olive oil
¼ cup water
½ cup white wine

Cut the lamb into 2½-inch squares and sprinkle with the salt, pepper, and rosemary. Put a piece of the onion and a little of the garlic on each square, roll it up, and secure it with toothpicks.

Brown the rolls in the oil, turning to brown evenly. After 3 or 4 minutes add the water; cover and steam for 10 minutes. Add the wine and simmer, uncovered, for 5 minutes longer.

Serves 6. About 250 calories each.

Lamb with Egg Sauce

Agnello alla Salsa di Uova

2 pounds lean lamb, cut into 1-inch cubes	½ cup water
½ teaspoon salt	½ teaspoon rosemary
¼ teaspoon pepper	1 clove garlic, crushed
flour	1 tablespoon lemon juice
1 tablespoon oil	¼ cup seasoned chicken broth
	2 egg yolks, beaten

Sprinkle the lamb with the salt and pepper and dust with the flour. Sauté in the oil, turning to brown evenly. Add the water, rosemary, and garlic. Cover and simmer for 30 minutes.

Combine the lemon juice and broth with the egg yolks. Simmer until thickened. Serve the lamb with the sauce poured over.

Serves 6. About 325 calories each.

Sweet and Sour Lamb

Agnello in Agrodolce

1½ pounds lean lamb, cut into 1-inch cubes	1 teaspoon salt
1 tablespoons olive oil	¼ teaspoon pepper
1 large onion, sliced thin	¼ cup pineapple chunks
2 teaspoons sugar	¼ cup tomatoes or 2 tablespoons tomato paste.
¼ cup vinegar	

Brown the lamb in the oil, turning to brown evenly. Add the onion and continue to brown, stirring frequently.

Meanwhile, combine the remaining ingredients and add to the lamb. Cover and simmer for 30 minutes until the meat is tender. Adjust the seasoning.

Serves 4. About 340 calories each.

Lamb with Fennel

Agnello con Finocchielli

2 fennel hearts
1½ pounds lean lamb
1 teaspoon salt
¼ teaspoon pepper
flour

2 tablespoons oil
2 tablespoons chopped onion
2 fresh or 1 cup peeled canned
  tomatoes
pinch sugar

Trim the fennel and cut the bulbs in half. Boil in water just to cover until almost tender, about 20 minutes.

Cut the lamb into about 1-inch cubes. Dust with the salt and pepper and very lightly with the flour. Brown in the oil, turning once or twice. Add the onion and sauté until transparent. Add the tomatoes and 1 cup of the water from the fennel. Simmer until tender, about 30 minutes.

Meanwhile, cut the fennel into large dice. Add to the lamb and reheat. If lamb is too dry, add more water from the fennel.

Serves 4. About 380 calories each.

Lamb Hunter's Style

Agnello alla Cacciatora

2 pounds lean leg of lamb, cut
  into 1-inch cubes
1 tablespoon flour
1 teaspoon salt
¼ teaspoon pepper

2 tablespoons oil
1 to 2 cloves garlic, crushed
1 teaspoon rosemary
½ cup water
½ cup white wine

Rub the lamb with the flour mixed with the salt and pepper. Brown in the oil, turning to brown evenly.

Add the garlic, rosemary, water, and wine. Cover tight and simmer until the meat is tender, about 30 minutes. Add more liquid if necessary. Adjust the seasoning.

Serves 6. About 255 calories each.

Lamb Stew with Zucchini

Agnello in Umido con Zucchini

1¼ pounds lean lamb, cut into 1-inch cubes
1 medium onion, chopped
2 tablespoons olive oil
1 clove garlic, crushed
1 large tomato, peeled and chopped

1 teaspoon salt
¼ teaspoon pepper
½ teaspoon oregano or rosemary
1½ pounds zucchini, cut in ½-inch rounds

Be sure to trim all the fat from the lamb. Brown the onion in the oil and add the lamb and garlic. Turn the lamb to brown evenly. Add the tomato, salt, pepper, and the herb. Cover and simmer for about 30 minutes.

Add the zucchini and cover and cook 8 to 10 minutes, until the squash is tender.

Serves 4. About 285 calories each.

Lamb with Capers

Agnello coi Capperi

2½ pounds lean lamb, cut into 1-inch cubes
1 tablespoon flour
1 teaspoon salt
¼ teaspoon pepper
1 tablespoon oil
1 tablespoon butter
1 medium onion, chopped
2 cloves garlic, minced

2 stalks celery, scraped and chopped
2 carrots, scraped and chopped
1 green pepper, seeded and chopped
1 cup water
1 can (8 ounces) tomatoes
¼ cup capers

Cut all the fat off the lamb and dust with the flour, salt, and pepper. Sauté in the oil and butter, stirring to brown evenly. Add the onion and garlic; stir and cook for 3 or 4 minutes.

Add the remaining ingredients except the capers. Cover and simmer until the lamb is tender, about 25 minutes. Add the capers and their liquid and simmer for 10 minutes.

Serves 6. About 325 calories each.

PORK

Pork is very popular in Italy; actually, more pork is eaten than any other meat. This is due to the use of pork in sausages, and cured, smoked, and salted pork. The many, many sausages include the well known *salame* and *mortadella di Bologna*. *Prosciutto* is the name for all ham, not only the Parma-cured variety.

The name *carne di maiale* (meat of the pig) comes from the goddess Maia, the mother of Mercury. The legend goes that when Aeneas landed in Italy he was about to sacrifice a sow. She got excited (and why not?) and gave birth to thirty piglets! This was considered to be a sign from the gods, and so pork came into fashion.

Pork Scallopine I

Scaloppine di Maiale I

1⅓ pounds pork tenderloin
1 tablespoon olive oil
1 clove garlic, crushed
1 teaspoon salt

¼ teaspoon pepper
½ teaspoon rosemary or ¼
  teaspoon sage
2 teaspoons lemon juice

Trim off any fat and cut the pork into ⅓-inch slices. Brown in the oil, turning once. Add the remaining ingredients, reduce the heat, and cook for about 20 minutes. If the pork sticks, add a tablespoon or two of water.

Serves 4. About 330 calories each.

Pork Scallopine II

Scaloppine di Maiale II

1½ pounds very lean pork, cut
   into thin slices
1 tablespoon olive oil or butter
1 clove garlic, chopped

2 tablespoons minced parsley
½ teaspoon salt
¼ teaspoon pepper
1 tablespoon lemon juice

Sauté the pork in the oil or butter, turning to brown evenly. Add the remaining ingredients and cook for 20 minutes, turning the slices frequently.

Serves 4. About 325 calories each.

Pork Cooked in Milk

Arrosto di Maiale al Latte

2 pounds lean, boned loin of
   pork
2 tablespoons butter
1 clove garlic, split

2 cups skim milk
1 teaspoon salt
¼ teaspoon pepper
2 to 3 teaspoons warm water

Be sure to trim the fat from the pork. If necessary, roll it and tie with string so it will keep its shape.

Brown lightly in the butter with the garlic on all sides. Remove the garlic and add the milk slowly; add the salt and pepper. Cover and simmer gently for about 1½ hours, until the meat is tender. Most of the milk will be absorbed.

Skim off all the excess fat. Add the water if needed and scrape up all the brown bits. Slice the pork thin and pour the sauce over.

Serves 6. About 350 calories each.

Pork Tenderloin in White Wine

Braciolino di Maiale al Vino Bianco

2 pounds pork tenderloin	2 tablespoons olive oil
1 clove garlic, crushed	½ cup broth
1 teaspoon salt	½ cup white wine

Pork tenderloin has almost no fat, but if it has, trim it off.

Cut into 6 pieces and flatten slightly. Rub with the garlic and salt. Sauté in the oil for 2 to 3 minutes to brown on both sides. Add the broth and wine. Cook uncovered for about 15 minutes, until the pork is tender and most of the liquid is absorbed.

Serves 6. About 350 calories each.

Roast Pork

Arrosto di Maiale

1 3-pound pork roast, preferably loin	1 teaspoon salt
2 cloves garlic, slivered	½ teaspoon pepper
	1 teaspoon rosemary

Preheat oven to 450°.

Remove all excess fat. Make tiny slits in the pork with a small knife and insert the slivers of garlic. Rub the roast with the salt, pepper, and rosemary. Roast for 15 minutes, reduce the heat to 350°, and roast for 1¼ to 1½ hours, turning the meat several times. Test for doneness. There should be no pink when a slit is made near the bone.

Serves 6. About 400 calories each.

Pan-Fried Pork Chops

Costolette di Maiale in Padella

The chops must be thin to be cooked this way.

8 pork chops, cut ¼ inch thick   ¼ teaspoon pepper
1 clove garlic, split   ½ teaspoon rosemary
1 teaspoon salt   1 tablespoon oil

Rub the chops on both sides with the garlic. Sprinkle with the salt, pepper, and rosemary and sauté in the oil to brown both sides. Reduce the heat and cook for about 10 minutes, turning several times, until no pink shows when the meat is slit with a sharp knife near the bone.

Serves 4. About 330 calories each.

Breaded Pork Chops

Costolette di Maiale Panate

8 pork chops, cut ¼ inch thick   ½ cup bread crumbs
½ cup flour   2 tablespoons olive oil
1 egg   1 teaspoon salt
2 tablespoons water   ¼ teaspoon pepper

Trim all the fat from the chops and roll them in flour. Beat the egg with the water. Dip the chops in the egg and then in the bread crumbs. Let stand for 15 minutes.

Fry in the oil for 2 minutes, turning to brown on both sides. Reduce the heat and continue to cook gently for 15 minutes, turning several times.

Serves 4. About 395 calories each.

Spare Ribs with Tomato Sauce

Costole di Maiale con Salsa di Pomidoro

3 pounds spare ribs   1 clove garlic, crushed
1 can (8 ounces) tomato sauce   ½ teaspoon salt
  or purée   ¼ teaspoon pepper
1 cup water

Preheat oven to 450°.

Have the ribs cut into serving pieces and trim off any

excess fat. Place in a roasting pan and bake for 15 minutes, turning once to brown both sides.

Mix the tomato sauce with the water, garlic, salt, and pepper and pour over. Reduce the heat to 325° and bake for about 1¼ hours, turning several times.

Serves 4. About 425 calories each.

Sausage and Peppers

Salsiccia con Peperoni

8 Italian sausages (about 1¼ pounds)
½ cup water
1 clove garlic, minced

4 green peppers, seeded and sliced into strips
½ cup tomato sauce

Brown the sausages in the water. Prick each one several times to release the fat. Add the garlic and peppers. Stir and cook for about 10 minutes; add the tomato sauce, cover, and cook gently for about 10 minutes more. Skim off excess fat.

Serves 4. About 300 calories each.

Sausages and Tomatoes

Salsiccia con Pomidoro

1¾ pounds sausages, cut in half
1 tablespoon olive oil
1 tablespoon water
1 clove garlic, minced

1 can (1 pound) peeled tomatoes
1 teaspoon salt
¼ teaspoon pepper
1 teaspoon sage

Brown the sausage in the oil and water; add the garlic and brown it. Add tomatoes and seasonings and simmer, covered, for 20 minutes. Skim off any fat.

Serves 6. About 275 calories each.

VARIETY MEATS

We seem to prefer the term "variety meats" to the more descriptive "innards" or "organs." Perhaps they taste better that way! Certainly there is a variety from which to choose, from liver, sweetbreads, and kidneys to the less popular tripe and brains.

Liver is extremely rich in iron and vitamins. In order to profit from this as well as from its flavor, you must serve it fresh or fresh-frozen, and never overcook it. The liver of a young calf is superior to that of a steer, lamb, or pig, although it can be used in some dishes. Venice is famous for its *fegato,* a combination of very thin slices of calves' liver, cooked quickly, and quantities of slowly sautéed onions. Chicken livers are much cheaper than calves' and are delicate and equally nutritious. When preparing chicken livers, it is necessary to cut off any greenish spots; if left on, they will give the dish a bitter taste.

Kidneys should be more popular than they are, and perhaps they would be if we called them *rognoni* and cooked them properly, that is, avoided overcooking them, which makes them tough. Veal and lamb kidneys are the best, the most tender and delicate.

Broiled Calves' Liver

Fegato di Vitello alla Griglia

1 pound calves' liver, sliced ½   ¼ teaspoon pepper
  inch thick   ½ tablespoon olive oil
½ teaspoon salt

Preheat broiler.

Sprinkle the liver with the salt and pepper and brush with the oil on both sides. Broil close to the heat — 3 or 4 inches — for 3 minutes; turn and broil for 2 minutes. Do not cook any longer or the liver will be tough.

Serves 4. About 185 calories each.

Calves' Liver in Mustard Sauce

Fegato di Vitello al Sugo di Senape

1 pound calves' liver, cut ¼ inch thick	1 tablespoon prepared mustard
2 tablespoons butter	¼ teaspoon salt
2 tablespoons strong broth	pinch sugar
⅓ cup cream	1 tablespoon minced parsley

Sauté the liver in the butter, turning once. The total cooking time should not exceed 3 minutes. Remove to a hot platter and keep warm.

Add the broth to the skillet and bring to a boil. Stir in the cream mixed with the mustard, salt, and sugar. Reduce the heat and simmer for a few minutes. Add the parsley and pour over the liver.

Serves 4. About 285 calories each.

Venetian Calves' Liver I

Fegato di Vitello alla Veneziana I

1½ pounds calves' liver, cut very thin, about ¼ inch thick or less	1 teaspoon salt
	½ teaspoon pepper
1 cup minced onions	1 teaspoon minced parsley or mint (garnish)
2 tablespoons olive oil	

Cut the liver into 2-inch squares. Sauté the onions very slowly in the oil for 5 minutes, stirring several times. Add the liver, salt, and pepper and cook for 2 or 3 minutes, turning to brown evenly. Serve at once, sprinkled with the parsley or mint.

Serves 6. About 200 calories each.

Venetian Calves' Liver II

Fegato di Vitello alla Veneziana II

2 onions, sliced thick
2 tablespoons olive oil
1 pound calves' liver, sliced thin

½ teaspoon salt
¼ teaspoon pepper
1 lemon, cut into wedges

Sauté the onions in the oil until browned. Add the liver and sprinkle with the salt and pepper. Cook over high heat to brown, about 2 minutes and no more than 3. Turn the liver once. It should be pink inside and tender. Serve with the lemon wedges.

Serves 4. About 240 calories each.

Calves' Liver with Tomatoes

Fegato di Vitello al Pomidoro

1 pound calves' liver, cut ¼ to
  ½ inch thick
flour
salt and pepper

1 clove garlic, crushed
2 tablespoons olive oil
1 can (15 ounces) tomato
  sauce

Dust the liver lightly with the flour and sprinkle with the salt and pepper. Sauté with the garlic in the oil for 2 minutes; turn and brown the other side. Add the tomato sauce and cook only for 1 or 2 minutes, until hot. Adjust the seasoning.

Serves 4. About 250 calories each.

Calves' Liver Milan Style I

Fegato di Vitello alla Milanese I

1 pound calves' liver, sliced ¼
  inch thick
1 teaspoon salt
½ teaspoon pepper
juice of 1 lemon
1 egg, beaten

1 teaspoon water
fine bread crumbs
2 tablespoons butter
1 tablespoon chopped parsley
lemon wedges

Sprinkle the liver with the salt and pepper and a little lemon juice and let stand for about 1 hour. Dip in the egg mixed with the water and dust lightly with the bread crumbs, shaking off any excess. Brown in the butter, turning once, for a total cooking time of 2 minutes. Drain on paper toweling. Serve with the parsley and lemon wedges.

Serves 4. About 285 calories each.

Calves' Liver Milan Style II

Fegato di Vitello alla Milanese II

2 pounds calves' liver, cut into
  pieces
1 teaspoon salt
¼ teaspoon pepper
2 tablespoons olive oil
2 onions, sliced thin

½ pound mushrooms, sliced
1 can (8 ounces) tomato
  purée
2 tablespoons water
¼ cup red wine

Sprinkle the liver with the salt and pepper and sauté in the oil for 2 minutes; remove and set aside.

Sauté the onions for 2 minutes. Add the mushrooms and sauté for 2 minutes. Add the tomato purée mixed with the water and the red wine and simmer for 3 minutes.

Return the liver to the pan and cook for 2 minutes only.

Serves 8. About 285 calories each.

Liver on a Skewer

Spiedini di Fegatoni

1½ pounds chicken livers or
  calves' liver
6 slices bacon

½ teaspoon salt
¼ teaspoon pepper
1 tablespoon oil or bacon fat

Preheat broiler.

If using calves' liver, have it sliced ½ inch thick and cut it into 1-inch squares. If using chicken livers, cut each one in half. Sprinkle with the salt and pepper.

Cut the bacon into 1-inch squares.

Alternately thread the liver and bacon loosely on 6 long or 12 short skewers. Brush the liver with oil or melted bacon fat.

Broil for 3 minutes about 4 inches from the heat. Brush with the drippings, turn, and broil 3 minutes more, brushing several times with drippings. The bacon should be crisp.

Serves 6. About 225 calories each.

Chicken Livers on a Skewer

Fegatini di Pollo alla Griglia

1 pound chicken livers	1 clove garlic, crushed
½ pound small mushrooms	1 teaspoon salt
4 slices bacon	2 tablespoons olive oil
12 small onions, parboiled	

Preheat broiler.

Cut the livers into 2 pieces at their natural division. Cut the mushrooms in half if very large. Cut the bacon into squares.

Alternate the livers, mushrooms, bacon, and onions on 6 long skewers. Add the garlic and salt to the oil and brush the livers and mushrooms with it.

Broil about 6 inches from the heat for 3 minutes; turn, brush with any remaining oil, and broil for 3 minutes more. Serve on the skewers.

Serves 6. About 235 calories each.

Chicken Livers with Green Peppers

Fegatini di Pollo con Peperoni

2 medium onions, chopped	2 tablespoons broth
2 tablespoons oil or chicken fat	2 tomatoes, peeled and
1¼ pounds chicken livers	chopped
1 tablespoon flour	1 teaspoon salt
2 medium green peppers,	½ teaspoon pepper
seeded and coarsely	½ teaspoon sugar
chopped	

Sauté the onions in the oil or fat until light brown. Cut the livers in half and add to the onions. Sauté for 3 minutes, turning to brown evenly. Stir in the flour and cook for 2 minutes.

Meanwhile, sauté the green peppers in the broth for 5 minutes; add the tomatoes, salt, pepper, and sugar. Cover and simmer for 10 minutes and add to the liver.

Reheat and season to taste.

Serves 4. About 265 calories each.

Chicken Livers with Tomato Sauce

Fegatini di Pollo con Salsa di Pomidoro

1 medium onion, chopped	½ teaspoon salt
2 tablespoons oil	1 can (8 ounces) tomato sauce
1 pound chicken livers, cut up	1 bay leaf or 3 sage leaves

Sauté the onion in the oil. Add the livers and salt and sauté for 3 minutes. Add the tomato sauce and bay or sage and simmer for 5 minutes.

Serves 4. About 225 calories each.

Chicken Livers with Marsala

Fegatini di Pollo alla Marsala

1 pound chicken livers	1 tablespoon butter
flour	1 tablespoon oil
½ teaspoon salt	¼ teaspoon dried sage
¼ teaspoon pepper	2 tablespoons Marsala

Cut the livers into 2 pieces at their natural division. Dust with the flour and sprinkle with the salt and pepper. Sauté in the butter and oil for 3 mintues while stirring. Add the sage and Marsala and simmer for 3 minutes, stirring a few times.

Serves 4. About 210 calories each.

Chicken Livers with Sage I
Fegatini di Pollo alla Salvia I

1 pound chicken livers	6 sage leaves
2 tablespoons minced onion	2 tablespoons butter
½ teaspoon salt	¼ cup white wine

Sauté the livers, onion, salt, and sage in the butter, stirring frequently for about 3 minutes. Remove to a warm plate. Add the wine to the pan and stir to scrape up any brown bits. Boil for 1 minute. Return the livers and any juice from the plate and heat. Adjust the seasoning.

Serves 4. About 220 calories each.

Chicken Livers with Sage II
Fegatini di Pollo alla Salvia II

1 medium onion, chopped fine	½ teaspoon salt
2 tablespoons butter	¼ teaspoon pepper
1 pound chicken livers	¼ cup broth
1 teaspoon sage	

Sauté the onion in the butter until light brown. Add the livers; stir and cook for 3 minutes. Add the sage, salt, and pepper and place on a hot platter.

Add the broth to the skillet and stir, scraping up any brown bits. Pour, boiling, over the livers or, if the livers have cooled, add them to the juices and reheat.

Serves 4. About 200 calories each.

Chicken Livers with Mushrooms I
Fegatini di Pollo ai Funghi I

1 pound chicken livers	1 teaspoon salt
¼ cup chopped onion	¼ teaspoon pepper
2 tablespoons butter	3 tablespoons broth
1 tablespoon oil	¼ cup white wine
1 pound small mushrooms	

Cut the livers in half along their natural division and sauté with the onion in the butter for 2 minutes, stirring once or twice. Add the whole mushrooms, salt, and pepper and sauté for 3 minutes. Add the broth and wine and simmer for 2 minutes.

Serves 4. About 240 calories each.

Chicken Livers with Mushrooms II

Fegatini di Pollo ai Funghi II

1 large onion, chopped
2 tablespoons butter or half
   olive oil, half butter
1 pound chicken livers
1 pound mushrooms, coarsely
   sliced

1 teaspoon salt
¼ teaspoon pepper
pinch oregano
½ cup red wine

Sauté the onion in butter or butter and oil for 2 minutes. Cut the livers in half at their natural division and add to the onion. Cook 2 minutes and add the mushrooms. Season with the salt, pepper, and oregano, stir gently and cook for 4 or 5 minutes. Add the red wine and cook for 2 minutes to boil off the alcohol.

Serves 4. About 240 calories each.

Chicken Giblet Stew

Umido di Rigaglie di Pollo

1 pound chicken gizzards
½ pound chicken hearts
1 onion, chopped
5 stalks celery, scraped and
   cut into 1-inch pieces
2 tablespoons butter
1 teaspoon salt

¼ teaspoon pepper
1 pound chicken livers, cut in
   half
2 tablespoons prosciutto or
   other ham, diced
1 can (8 ounces) tomato paste

Cook the gizzards and hearts in lightly salted water just to cover until almost tender, about 45 minutes. Cool the gizzards and cut into 3 pieces, removing the gristle.

Meanwhile, sauté the onion and celery in the butter until the onion is transparent. Add the water from the gizzards, cover, and simmer for 10 minutes.

Add the gizzards, hearts, salt, pepper, and livers. Stir in the ham and tomato paste and simmer, covered, for 15 minutes.

Serves 6. About 290 calories each.

Broiled Kidneys

Rognoni alla Griglia

2 pounds veal or lamb kidneys	¼ teaspoon pepper
2 tablespoons melted butter	2 tablespoons minced parsley
½ teaspoon salt	(garnish)

Preheat broiler.

Cut the kidneys in half lengthwise and remove the center hard core and any membrane or fat. Brush with the melted butter and broil about 4 inches from the heat for 5 minutes. Sprinkle with half the salt and pepper, brush with butter, and turn. Add the remaining salt and pepper, brush with butter, and broil for 3 minutes.

Do not overcook or you will toughen the kidneys. Serve sprinkled with parsley.

Serves 6. About 230 calories each.

Kidneys with Mushrooms

Rognoni ai Funghi

4 veal or 8 lamb kidneys, about 1¼ pounds	½ pound mushrooms, sliced
	½ teaspoon lemon juice
1 clove garlic, crushed	1 teaspoon salt
1 tablespoon oil	½ teaspoon pepper
1 tablespoon butter	1 tablespoon minced parsley

Cut the kidneys in half and remove the hard center core and any membrane. Slice them thin; sauté with the garlic in the oil and butter for 4 minutes while stirring. Add the mushrooms and cook for 2 or 3 minutes more. Add the lemon juice, salt, pepper, and parsley. Adjust the seasoning.

Serves 4. About 245 calories each.

Kidneys in Mustard Sauce

Rognoni al Sugo con Senape

6 or 8 veal kidneys or 12 to 15 lamb, about 2 pounds
1 teaspoon salt
¼ teaspoon pepper
2 tablespoons butter

1 tablespoon flour
1 tablespoon prepared mustard
½ cup broth or water
½ cup cream or sour cream

Remove the center core and all the membrane from the kidneys and slice thin. Sprinkle with the salt and pepper and sauté in the butter for 5 minutes. Combine the flour and mustard and add to the kidneys. Add the broth or water and simmer and stir. Reduce the heat and stir in the cream or sour cream. Heat and serve at once.

Serves 6. About 300 calories each.

Kidneys in White Wine

Rognoni al Vino Bianco

1¼ pounds veal or lamb kidneys
1 pound onions, sliced

1 tablespoon butter
¼ cup broth
½ cup white wine

Cut the kidneys in half to remove the center core and any membranes. Slice them thin. Sauté the onions for 1 minute in the butter; add the broth and simmer until softened, not brown. Add the kidneys, stir and cook for 1 minute; add half the wine, cover, and simmer for 5 minutes. Add more wine as needed.

Serves 4. About 240 calories each.

Kidneys in Red Wine

Rognoni al Vino Rosso

8 lamb or 4 veal kidneys, about 1¼ pounds	1 teaspoon salt
1 medium onion, sliced thin	¼ teaspoon pepper
1 clove garlic, minced	½ cup red wine
2 tablespoons butter or oil	1 tablespoon minced parsley (garnish)

Cut the kidneys in half to remove the hard center core and any membranes. Slice about ½ inch thick. Sauté the onion and garlic in the butter for 1 minute; add the kidneys and sauté for about 10 minutes. Season with the salt and pepper, add the wine, and simmer to reduce, about 2 minutes or so. Serve topped with parsley.

Serves 4. About 270 calories each.

Veal Kidneys on a Skewer

Spiedini di Rognoni di Vitello

2 pounds veal kidneys	1 clove garlic, crushed
2 tablespoons melted butter	1 tablespoon minced parsley
¼ cup beef broth	
1 tablespoon prepared mustard	

Cut the kidneys in half and remove the hard center core. Thread the kidneys on 6 large skewers. Place in a broiler pan.

Combine the remaining ingredients, brush the kidneys with the marinade, turn, and pour the remaining marinade over. Let sit in the refrigerator for 1 hour or more.

Preheat broiler.

Broil for 5 minutes on each side, basting frequently with the marinade. Serve with any remaining marinade and juices poured over. Don't overcook!

Serves 6. About 215 calories each.

Beef Kidney Stew

Rognoni di Manzo in Umido

2 pounds beef kidneys
juice of 1 lemon
2 tablespoons oil
1 clove garlic, minced
3 onions, chopped
1 cup canned or 3 fresh
  tomatoes, peeled

1 teaspoon salt
½ teaspoon pepper
½ cup broth
¼ cup wine, red or white

Quarter the kidneys; remove the center core and any membrane or fat. Beef kidneys have a stronger flavor than veal or lamb and are improved by being plunged into boiling water, with lemon juice, to cover. Let stand a few minutes to cool and then pat dry.

Slice the kidneys thin and sauté in the oil with the garlic and onion for 3 minutes. Add the tomatoes, salt, pepper, and broth and simmer for 5 minutes. Add the wine and cook for 2 minutes. Don't overcook the kidneys or they will be tough.

Serves 6. About 265 calories each.

SWEETBREADS

Sweetbreads, *animelle*, are the thymus gland situated in the neck of young animals — calves, lambs, and pigs. Pig sweetbreads have a strong, rather unpleasant flavor, and lamb sweetbreads are small and difficult to handle; they are used in Italy more than they are here. Calves' sweetbreads are delicate and delicious. The thymus gland disappears as the animal reaches maturity, so there are no real mutton or beef sweetbreads.

The advance preparation remains the same regardless of how you cook them. Be sure the sweetbreads are fresh. Soak them in 1 quart of cold water with 1 tablespoon of lemon juice for about 1 hour, then simmer gently in fresh water with a little salt for about 15 minutes. Drain and plunge into ice water. When cool, they will be firm enough so that the membranes can be pulled off. Lamb sweetbreads are treated the same way except that they are simmered for only a minute or two.

Sautéed Sweetbreads

Animelle Sauté

1¼ pounds sweetbreads
2 tablespoons flour
1 teaspoon salt

¼ teaspoon pepper
3 tablespoons butter

Prepare the sweetbreads as directed above. Cut each piece into 2 or 3 slices. Dust with a mixture of the flour, salt, and pepper. Brown in the hot butter for 2 or 3 minutes on each side. Serve at once.

Serves 4. About 200 calories each.

Fried Sweetbreads

Animelle Fritte

1¾ pounds sweetbreads
1 egg
1 teaspoon salt
¼ teaspoon pepper
2 tablespoons fine dry bread
  crumbs

2 tablespoons grated
  Parmesan cheese (optional)
3 tablespoons butter or oil

Prepare the sweetbreads as directed on page 195. Slice them into pieces about ¾ inch thick. Beat the egg with the salt and pepper. Dip the sweetbreads in the egg and then into the crumbs (mixed with the cheese, if you wish). Fry them in the hot butter or oil, turning to brown on both sides. Serve with the butter poured over.

Serves 6. About 200 calories each; 235 with Parmesan cheese.

Creamed Sweetbreads

Animelle con Sugo di Panne

1¼ pounds sweetbreads
2 tablespoons butter
2 tablespoons flour
1 cup light cream
½ cup chicken broth

1 tablespoon minced parsley
1 teaspoon salt
¼ teaspoon white pepper
pinch rosemary or marjoram

Prepare the sweetbreads as directed on page 195. Break or cut them into small pieces. Melt the butter, blend in the flour, and add the cream and broth slowly while stirring. When the liquid is slightly thickened, reduce the heat and add the remaining ingredients. Stir gently and simmer for about 5 minutes.

If the sauce is too thin, add a little flour and milk paste.

Serves 4. About 300 calories each.

Sweetbreads Sautéed with Marsala

Animelle alla Marsala

1¼ pounds sweetbreads
1 teaspoon salt
¼ teaspoon pepper

3 tablespoons butter
½ cup Marsala

Prepare the sweetbreads as directed on page 195. Slice them and sprinkle with the salt and pepper. Brown in the butter for about 3 minutes on each side. Pour in the wine and boil for 2 minutes. Serve with the juices poured over.

Serves 4. About 200 calories each.

Lamb Sweetbreads with Mushrooms

Animelle di Agnello di Funghi

1¼ pounds lamb sweetbreads
2 tablespoons butter
1 tablespoon minced onions
¼ pound mushrooms, sliced
   thin

2 tablespoons sherry, Marsala, or white wine

Prepare the sweetbreads as directed on page 195 and slice. Sauté them in the butter with the onions and mushrooms. Stir and cook gently for about 5 minutes until lightly browned. Add the wine and simmer for 2 minutes. Serve with the juices poured over.

Serves 4. About 210 calories each.

Vegetables

THE ITALIANS PREFER their vegetables, as they do their pasta, at the *al dente* stage. They must not be mushy.

Fresh vegetables in season are the best, topped only by the Italian baby first-of-the-crop ones — *primizie*.

If what you want is not in season, do not be afraid to use frozen vegetables. Having been frozen at the peak of their careers, they are better than the limp, tired ones that have been shipped long distances. A few canned vegetables are acceptable. One of these, fortunately, is the tomato; the peeled Italian plum tomato is most useful in Italian cookery.

Many vegetables are improved by adding herbs, a clove of garlic, and some lemon juice or wine to the liquid in which they are cooked, or by substituting broth for water. Prepared this way, many do not require butter to make them delicious. Served as a separate course, vegetables became invaluable in low-calorie Italian cookery.

ARTICHOKES

In Italy, the "choke" is almost always removed before the artichoke (*carciofo*) is served. In the United States, the diner is usually expected to scrape out his own after nibling the ends off the leaves. If you are serving Italian style, remove the choke after the vegetable has been cooked, which is easier to do than when it is raw. Spread the leaves apart and scoop out the thistlelike center with a teaspoon. Push the leaves back into place and serve it hot with melted butter and a dash of lemon juice or cold with vinaigrette sauce.

Steamed Artichokes

Carciofi

4 artichokes	1 tablespoon salt
¼ cup vinegar	¼ cup melted butter

Cut off the bottom of the stem and pull off the small outside leaves from the bottom. You may cut the ends of the leaves, which makes the artichokes more attractive and easier to eat, but it does not affect the flavor. Certainly trim any discolored leaves.

Place in a steamer or in a large pot with a tight-fitting lid, add the vinegar and the salt to the water to cover. Cover and steam for about 35 minutes, until a leaf pulls out easily. Remove with tongs and drain upside down. Serve with 1 tablespoon butter for each person to dip the ends of the leaves into.

Serves 4. About 150 calories each.

Artichokes Roman Style

Carciofi alla Romana

6 young artichokes	½ teaspoon salt
½ cup bread crumbs	½ teaspoon pepper
1 large clove garlic, minced	3 anchovies, chopped
juice of ½ lemon	3 tablespoons olive oil
3 tablespoons minced parsley	1 cup water
½ teaspoon marjoram or basil	

Prepare the artichokes as for Steamed Artichokes*, removing the choke while raw. Spread the leaves apart by pressing them down on a table. Combine the bread crumbs with the garlic, lemon juice, parsley, marjoram or basil, salt, pepper, and anchovies. Divide this mixture among the artichokes, putting it inside and pressing the leaves back into place.

Stand the artichokes side by side in a pot with a tight-fitting lid. Pour the oil and water over. Cover and steam for about 25 minutes. Remove the lid and cook for 10 minutes more. The artichokes are done when a leaf pulls out easily.

Serves 6. About 180 calories each.

Asparagus with Lemon

Asparagi al Limone

1¾ pounds asparagus
1 teaspoon salt
1 tablespoon butter

2 tablespoons lemon juice
½ teaspoon salt

Cut off the tough ends of the asparagus and scrape the stems up several inches with a vegetable scraper. Put into a steamer or a pot deep enough to permit the asparagus to stand up. If using a steamer, steam over boiling salted water until almost tender, 15 or 20 minutes. If using a pot, add 3 inches of water, tie the asparagus in 4 bunches, and stand in the pot; cover tight and cook until tender, 15 to 20 minutes.

Melt the butter, add the lemon juice and salt, and heat. Place the asparagus on a warm serving dish or 4 hot plates and pour the very hot liquid over.

Serves 4. About 48 calories each.

Asparagus with Butter

Asparagi al Burro

3 pounds asparagus
1 teaspoon salt
3 tablespoons melted butter

2 tablespoons Parmesan
cheese (optional)

Break off the tough ends of the asparagus and discard. Scrape the stems about halfway up with a vegetable peeler. Put into a steamer or use a deep pot and stand the asparagus in 2 inches of water. Cover tight and steam until crisp-tender, about 10 to 15 minutes; the cooking time depends on the thickness of the stalks. Sprinkle with the salt and pour the butter over. Sprinkle cheese on top, if you wish.

Serves 6. About 85 calories each; 110 with cheese.

Baked Asparagus

Asparagi al Forno

2 pounds asparagus	1 teaspoon salt
1 tablespoon melted butter	¼ teaspoon pepper
1 tablespoon olive oil	1 tablespoon minced parsley
1 tablespoon lemon juice	

Preheat oven to 400°.

Wash the asparagus, cut off the tough ends, and scrape 2 or 3 inches up the stems. Place in a shallow baking dish, preferably Pyrex. Pour over the remaining ingredients. Cover with foil and bake until tender, about 25 minutes.

Serves 4. About 85 calories each.

BEANS

There are many varieties of beans. *Fagiolini verde* are green beans, the kind we used to call "string beans." Broadbeans, which have to be shelled, are *fava,* and dried beans, which need to be soaked, are *fagioti.* In this book the emphasis is on green beans, since they are much lower in calories than the starchy ones.

Green Beans

Fagiolini

1 pound green beans	4 tablespoons Low-Calorie
1 teaspoon salt	Italian-Type Dressing*,
¼ teaspoon pepper	warmed

Cut or French-cut the beans unless they are very young, in which case leave them whole and tie together loosely with a piece of string. Put into a pot with the salt, pepper, and boiling water almost to cover. Cover and simmer until tender, 15 to 20 minutes. Drain and pour the dressing over.

Serves 4. About 40 calories each.

Green Beans and Tomatoes

Fagiolini con Pomidori

2 packages (10 ounces each)	¼ teaspoon pepper
frozen cut green beans	2 teaspoons Worcestershire
1 can (10 ounces) tomatoes	sauce
1 onion, minced	2 tablespoons minced parsley
1 teaspoon salt	

Cook the beans according to the package directions, cooking a little less than the time indicated. Drain and add the tomatoes and the remaining ingredients. Cover and simmer for 10 minutes.

Serves 6. About 40 calories each.

Wax or Green Beans in Broth

Fagiolini in Brodo

1½ pounds fresh or 2	½ teaspoon salt
packages (10 ounces each)	¼ teaspoon sugar
frozen wax or green beans	1 large tomato, peeled and
1 cup broth	chopped
1 clove garlic, crushed	1 tablespoon minced parsley

Trim the ends of the beans and cut into 1-inch pieces. Cook in the broth with the garlic for 10 minutes. Add the remaining ingredients and cover and cook for 10 minutes. If using frozen beans, follow the package directions, using broth in place of water and adding all of the remaining ingredients as soon as the beans are thawed.

Serves 6. About 50 calories each.

Green Beans with Tomato Sauce

Fagiolini Verdi all'Argentina

1 clove garlic, crushed
3 tablespoons chopped onion
2 tablespoons olive oil
1 pound tomatoes, peeled
1 pound green beans, cut into
   1-inch pieces, or 2 packages
   (10 ounces each) frozen cut
   beans

1 teaspoon salt
¼ teaspoon pepper
pinch sugar

Sauté the garlic and onion in the oil until light brown. Add the tomatoes and beans, season with the salt, pepper, and sugar, and add water almost to cover. Cover and simmer for 30 minutes, stirring several times. Adjust the seasoning and pour off any excess liquid.

Serves 6. About 70 calories each.

Broadbeans with Bacon

Fava con Guanciale

1 pound broadbeans, shelled
3 slices bacon
1 medium onion, chopped

2 tablespoons broth
½ teaspoon salt
¼ teaspoon pepper

Shell the beans. Fry the bacon until it wilts; add the onion and brown for 2 or 3 minutes. Add the beans, broth, salt, and pepper. Cover and simmer until the beans are tender, about 20 minutes.

Serves 6. About 200 calories each.

Broccoli with Olive Oil

Broccoli all'Agro

1 bunch broccoli, about 1 pound	1 tablespoon lemon juice
	2 tablespoons olive oil
1 teaspoon salt	½ teaspoon oregano

Divide the broccoli head into flowerets. Peel the stems, discarding the tough ends. Cut the stem pieces into ½-inch lengths and put into a pot with water almost to cover and the salt. Cover and cook until the stem pieces are almost tender, about 5 minutes; add the flowerets and cook for 8 minutes longer. Drain and dress with the lemon juice, olive oil, and oregano.

Serves 4. About 80 calories each.

Broccoli with Lemon

Broccoli al Limone

1 bunch broccoli, about 1½ pounds	1 tablespoon olive oil
	2 tablespoons lemon juice
1½ teaspoons salt	¼ teaspoon pepper

Cut off the tough ends of the broccoli stalks and scrape or peel off the hard skins on the stems. Split the stalks or, if very large, cut in quarters. Boil in water barely to cover with 1 teaspoon of the salt, or steam over water, until tender, about 8 minutes. Drain and place on a hot serving dish and keep hot. Heat the oil, lemon juice, remaining ½ teaspoon salt, and pepper and pour over.

Serves 4. About 75 calories each.

Broccoli Roman Style

Broccoli alla Romana

2 pounds broccoli
2 tablespoons olive oil
1 clove garlic, crushed
¼ cup water

¼ cup white wine
3 anchovies, minced, or 1
    teaspoon anchovy paste

Cut off the tough stems and leaves of the broccoli and discard. Divide the stalks into serving-size pieces. If the stems are heavy, peel with a vegetable peeler and make a cross in the bottom of each stem with a sharp knife.

Brush the broccoli with the oil and with garlic. Sauté and stir for 5 minutes; add the water and wine, cover, and simmer until tender, about 15 minutes. Add the anchovies and simmer, uncovered, for 5 minutes.

Serves 6. About 95 calories each.

Broccoli with Mustard Sauce

Broccoli con Salsa di Senape

2 pounds fresh or 3 packages
    (10 ounces each) frozen
    broccoli
2 tablespoons minced onion
2 tablespoons butter
2 tablespoons flour
1 cup skim milk

2 tablespoons prepared
    mustard
1 teaspoon salt
¼ teaspoon pepper
1 teaspoon sugar
1 tablespoon lemon juice

Trim the broccoli and scrape the stems. Cook in salted water until tender, about 10 minutes. If using frozen broccoli, cook according to the package directions. Don't overcook. Sauté the onions in the butter, blend in the flour, and pour in the milk slowly while stirring. Blend in the mustard and add the salt, pepper, and sugar. Cook and stir until thickened and then add the lemon juice.

Drain the broccoli and pour the sauce over.

Serves 6. About 97 calories each.

Broccoli Purée

Purè di Broccoli

2 bunches fresh or 3 packages (10 ounces each) frozen broccoli
2 tablespoons butter or olive oil

1 teaspoon salt
¼ teaspoon pepper
1 clove garlic, crushed

Cut the stems from the broccoli and cook in salted water until soft; add the flowerets and cook 5 or 6 minutes more. If using frozen broccoli, follow the package directions but cook 2 or 3 extra minutes. Purée in a blender or food processor with a little of the water it was cooked in. Reheat with the remaining ingredients.
Serves 6. About 80 calories each.

Carrots with Lemon

Carote al Limone

1½ pounds carrots, scraped and sliced thin
1 tablespoon butter
2 tablespoons lemon juice

½ teaspoon salt
¼ teaspoon pepper
½ teaspoon sugar
¼ teaspoon grated lemon rind

Cook the carrots in water almost to cover for 10 minutes. Drain off most of the liquid and add the remaining ingredients. Heat for several minutes and taste for seasoning.
Serves 4. About 65 calories each.

Carrot Purée

Purè di Carote

2½ pounds carrots
2 teaspoons salt
2 teaspoons sugar
2 tablespoons frozen orange juice concentrate

grated rind of 1 orange
2 tablespoons any orange-flavored liqueur: Triple Sec, Grand Marnier, Cointreau, etc.

Scrape the carrots, slice, and cook them in water to cover with the salt and sugar. Cook until they are quite tender, about 20 to 30 minutes. Purée in a blender or food processor with the orange juice, rind, and the liqueur. Adjust the seasoning. Reheat.

Serves 6. About 75 calories each.

Boiled or Steamed Cauliflower

Cavolfiore Bollito

1 head cauliflower, about 2 pounds	¼ teaspoon pepper
1 teaspoon lemon juice	2 tablespoons butter or 3 tablespoons Low-Calorie
1 teaspoon salt	Italian-Type Dressing*

Cook the cauliflower in water to cover with the remaining ingredients except the butter or dressing. Cook until tender, about 20 minutes. If you steam it, add the seasonings after draining; it will take about 25 minutes to cook. If you break it into flowerets, cut the cooking time in half.

Serves 6. About 75 calories each with butter; about 45 calories with the low-calorie dressing.

Cauliflower with Tomato Sauce

Cavolfiore al Sugo di Pomidoro

1 medium head cauliflower	2 teaspoons flour
1 teaspoon salt	½ teaspoon pepper
¼ cup minced onion	1 can (1 pound) Italian
chicken broth	tomatoes

Break the cauliflower into flowerets and cook in salted water almost to cover. Cook until just tender, about 12 minutes.

Meanwhile, sauté the onion in the broth until light

brown. Stir in the flour and pepper and then the tomatoes, stirring constantly. Continue to simmer for 10 minutes, stirring several times. Put the cauliflower into a heated serving dish and pour the sauce over.

Serves 4. About 60 calories each.

Cauliflower Baked with Cheese

Cavolfiore Gratinato al Formaggio

1 head cauliflower, about 2 pounds	¼ cup grated Parmesan cheese
1 teaspoon salt	1 tablespoon butter

Preheat oven to 375°.

Break the cauliflower into flowerets and cook in deep water until almost tender, about 10 minutes. Remove and put into a baking dish in one layer. Sprinkle with the salt and cheese and dot with the butter. Bake until the top is light brown, about 15 to 20 minutes.

Serves 6. About 140 calories each.

Celery with Tomatoes

Sedani coi Pomidori

1 onion, chopped	½ teaspoon sugar
2 tablespoons broth	¼ teaspoon pepper
1 green pepper, chopped	¼ teaspoon basil
1 can (8 ounces) Italian tomatoes	8 to 10 stalks celery, scraped and cut into 1-inch pieces
1 teaspoon salt	

Sauté the onion gently in the broth for 2 or 3 minutes while stirring. Add the remaining ingredients. Cover and simmer until the celery is tender, about 15 minutes.

Serves 4. About 55 calories each.

Stuffed Eggplant

Melanzane Ripiene

1 large or 2 medium eggplants
½ pound mushrooms, chopped
3 tablespoons minced onions
1 tablespoon minced parsley
2 large tomatoes, seeded and
   chopped, or ¾ cup canned
   Italian plum tomatoes

1 teaspoon oregano
½ teaspoon salt
¼ teaspoon pepper
2 tablespoons oil or butter

Preheat oven to 350°.

Bake the eggplant until tender, about 20 to 25 minutes. Remove and, when cool enough to handle, cut in half if medium sized, into quarters if large. Scoop out the flesh, reserving the shells. Chop the flesh and mix with the remaining ingredients except the oil. Simmer for 5 minutes.

Fill the eggplant shells, top with the oil or butter, and bake for 10 minutes.

Serves 4. About 100 calories each.

Grilled Eggplant

Melanzane in Gratella

2 medium-small eggplants
1 teaspoon salt
¼ teaspoon pepper

2 tablespoons oil
1 clove garlic, crushed

Preheat oven to 350°.

Cut the eggplants in half lengthwise; do not peel. Make some slashes crosswise in the flesh with a sharp knife. Sprinkle with the salt and pepper. Add the oil mixed with the garlic. Place skin side down in a baking dish. Cover with foil and bake until soft, about 30 minutes. Uncover and cook 10 minutes more.

Serves 4. About 65 calories each.

Stewed Eggplant with Tomatoes

Melanzane in Umido coi Pomidori

2 medium eggplants, peeled
2 tablespoons butter
1 small onion, chopped
1 clove garlic, crushed
1 tablespoon olive oil
3 large tomatoes, peeled and
  chopped, or 1 can (16
  ounces) peeled Italian
  tomatoes

1 teaspoon salt
½ teaspoon pepper
½ teaspoon sugar

Slice or cube the eggplants into serving pieces and sauté them gently in the butter.

Meanwhile, sauté the onion and garlic in the oil until soft, not brown. Add the tomatoes, salt, pepper, and sugar and simmer for 10 minutes, stirring several times. Pour over the eggplant and reheat.

Serves 6. About 95 calories each.

Sweet and Sour Eggplant

Caponata alla Siciliana

3 medium eggplants, peeled
¼ cup olive oil
2 onions, sliced thin
3 tablespoons minced parsley
2 stalks celery, scraped and
  sliced
2 large ripe olives, coarsely
  chopped

½ cup tomato purée
3 tablespoons red wine
  vinegar
2 tablespoons sugar
½ teaspoon salt
¼ teaspoon pepper
½ teaspoon oregano

Slice the eggplant, sprinkle with salt, and let drain for about 20 minutes. Scrape, rinse, and dice the eggplant and sauté it in 3 tablespoons of the oil until almost soft.

Add the remaining oil and sauté the onions until soft,

not brown.   Add the celery, olives, tomato purée, vinegar, and sugar.   Cover and simmer for 10 minutes. Watch it carefully, as the tomato purée tends to stick. Add a teaspoon or two of water if necessary.

Season with the salt, pepper, and oregano.   Cook for 10 more minutes, stirring frequently.

Serves 6.   About 180 calories each.

Escarole

Scarole

2 pounds escarole, chopped	¼ teaspoon salt
¼ cup beef broth	¼ teaspoon paprika
1 clove garlic, crushed	¼ teaspoon thyme
2 tablespoons chopped parsley	2 tablespoons butter (optional)

Combine all of the ingredients in a saucepan and cook over low heat for 15 minutes, stirring from time to time. Stir in the butter if you wish.

Serves 4.   About 30 calories each; about 80 calories with butter.

Fennel

Finocchio

3 large heads fennel	3 tablespoons broth
2 tablespoons butter	1 tablespoon minced parsley

Trim the fennel and quarter lengthwise.   Cook in salted water for about 20 to 25 minutes, until tender.   Drain, return to the pot with the butter, broth, and parsley, and boil for a few minutes to reduce the broth.

Serves 6.   About 75 calories each.

Sautéed Fennel

Finocchio alla Sautè

3 small or medium fennel bulbs	3 tablespoons butter
½ cup broth	½ teaspoon salt
1 cup water	¼ teaspoon pepper

Trim off the outer tough leaves and quarter the hearts. Boil in a mixture of the broth and water until tender, about 10 minutes. Drain.

Melt the butter and brown the fennel for 3 or 4 minutes with the salt and pepper. Add a tablespoon or two of water if necessary. The fennel should look glazed.

Serves 4. About 100 calories each.

Braised Fennel

Finocchio Cotto

2 large or 3 medium fennel bulbs	1 clove garlic, minced
2 tablespoons butter or olive oil or a mixture of the two	½ teaspoon salt
1 teaspoon lemon juice	¼ teaspoon pepper
	1 tablespoon minced parsley

Slice the fennel, removing any tough outer leaves. Put into a deep skillet with the remaining ingredients and cook gently until the fennel is tender, about 25 minutes.

Serves 4. About 75 calories each.

Baked Fennel au Gratin

Finocchio alla Parmigiana

3 large bulbs fennel	2 tablespoons melted butter
1 teaspoon salt	2 tablespoons grated Parmesan cheese
½ teaspoon pepper	

Preheat oven to 425°.

Trim the fennel, quarter the bulbs, and boil in water to cover for about 8 minutes. Drain, place in a baking dish, and season with the salt and pepper. Pour the butter over and sprinkle with the cheese. Bake until heated through and the cheese is lightly browned, about 15 minutes.

Serves 6. About 100 calories each.

Mushrooms with Garlic

Funghi all'Aglio

2 cloves garlic, minced or crushed
2 tablespoons olive oil
1 pound mushrooms, sliced

1 teaspoon oregano
½ teaspoon salt
¼ teaspoon pepper
2 tablespoons water

Sauté the garlic in the oil until it browns slightly; add the mushrooms and sauté for 2 minutes, while stirring. Add the remaining ingredients. Cover and steam for 2 minutes. Serve the mushrooms with their juice.

Serves 4. About 95 calories each.

Thin-Sliced Mushrooms

Funghi Trifolati

1 clove garlic, minced
1½ pounds mushrooms, sliced thin

3 tablespoons herb broth
2 tablespoons minced parsley
juice ½ lemon

Sauté the garlic in 1 tablespoon of the broth for 1 minute. The mushrooms should be sliced very thin through caps and stems. Add to the pan; stir and add the remaining broth and sauté for 2 or 3 minutes. Add the parsley and lemon juice, stir, and remove from heat. Serve at once with their juices.

Serves 6. About 70 calories each.

Frozen Peas with Butter

Pisellini al Burro I

1 small onion or 3 scallions,
  slivered
3 or 4 outside lettuce leaves
2 tablespoons butter

2 packages (10 ounces each)
  frozen tiny peas
1 teaspoon salt
½ teaspoon sugar

Heat the onion and lettuce leaves in the butter; do not brown. Add the peas, salt, and sugar. Simmer for about 10 minutes, 3 minutes after the peas are thawed and start to cook.

Serves 6. About 100 calories each.

Fresh Peas with Butter

Pisellini al Burro II

Proceed as in Frozen Peas with Butter*, using 3 pounds of fresh young peas instead of frozen. The total cooking time is 10 to 15 minutes, depending upon the size of the peas.

Serves 6. About 115 calories each.

Green Peas with Ham

Pisellini al Prosciutto

3 pounds fresh peas or 2
  packages (10 ounces each)
  frozen
¼ cup chopped prosciutto or
  other ham

1 clove garlic, crushed
3 tablespoons water
2 tablespoons olive oil
½ teaspoon salt
1 teaspoon sugar

Put all of the ingredients into a casserole or pot, cover, and simmer for 5 minutes. If using frozen peas, proceed the same way. Test the peas for doneness and adjust seasoning to taste.

Serves 6. About 280 calories each.

Fried Green Peppers

Peperoni Fritti

6 large green peppers, about 2 pounds
1 clove garlic, crushed or minced

2 tablespoons olive oil
½ teaspoon salt
¼ teaspoon pepper
1 tablespoon minced parsley

Remove the seeds from the peppers and cut the skin lengthwise into strips about 1 inch wide. Heat the olive oil in a skillet and add the garlic. Add the peppers and sauté for about 5 minutes, turning to brown evenly. Add the salt, pepper, and parsley; cover and cook over low heat until the peppers are tender, about 10 minutes.
Serves 6. About 55 calories each.

Green Peppers with Onions

Peperoni con Cipolle

6 large green peppers, seeded
2 tablespoons olive oil
2 medium onions, sliced thin

1 clove garlic, crushed
½ teaspoon salt
¼ teaspoon pepper

Cut the peppers lengthwise into strips 1 inch wide. Put into a skillet with the oil, onions, and garlic. Sauté and stir for 5 minutes, until the onion is lightly browned. Add the salt and pepper, cover, and cook slowly until the peppers are tender, about 10 minutes.
Serves 6. About 90 calories each.

Mashed Potatoes

Purè di Patate

6 large potatoes
3 tablespoons melted butter
⅓ cup hot milk
1 teaspoon salt

2 eggs (optional)
¼ cup grated Parmesan cheese (optional)

Boil the potatoes with their jackets on until tender, about 30 minutes. Peel as soon as they are cool enough to handle. Put through a ricer or sieve or beat with an electric mixer. Beat in the butter; add the very hot milk a little at a time, beating steadily. The amount of milk depends on the quality of the potatoes and on how soft you want them. Season with salt to taste.

If you want a yellow-looking purée, add the beaten eggs while heating over boiling water. If you like cheese, beat in the Parmesan in place of the eggs. In any case, keep the potatoes hot over boiling water or very low heat.

Serves 6. About 150 calories each; with eggs or cheese, about 200 calories each.

Herbed Mashed Potatoes

Purè di Patate all'Erbe

4 large potatoes
1 clove garlic, minced
½ teaspoon rosemary
½ teaspoon thyme
1 tablespoon minced parsley

1 tablespoon butter
1 teaspoon salt
¼ teaspoon white pepper
¼ to ⅓ cup hot milk

Boil the potatoes until quite tender, about 35 minutes. Peel and either rice them or mash. Add the remaining ingredients, except the milk, and whip. Continue to whip while adding the milk. Stop when the potatoes are the consistency you want. Adjust the seasoning.

Serves 4. About 130 calories each.

Stuffed Baked Potatoes

Patate Ripiene

2 large baking potatoes
¼ cup melted butter
1 teaspoon grated onion

1 teaspoon salt
¼ teaspoon pepper
¼ cup milk

Preheat oven to 400°.

Scrub and bake the potatoes until very soft, about 45 minutes. When they are cool enough to handle, cut them in half lengthwise and scoop out the flesh into a bowl. Set the shells aside.

Mix the potatoes with the butter, onion, salt, and pepper. Whip in the milk gradually. When fluffy, refill the potato half shells and bake for 15 minutes or put under the broiler for 8 to 10 minutes, until lightly browned on top.

Serves 4. About 165 calories each.

Variations

Herbed Stuffed Potatoes
Patate Ripiene all'Erbe

Add 1 clove garlic, crushed; 1 teaspoon mint; 1 tablespoon minced parsley; and a pinch of nutmeg to the potatoes and proceed as for Stuffed Baked Potatoes*.

Serves 4. About 165 calories each.

Stuffed Potatoes with Cheese
Patate Ripiene alla Ricotta

Add 3 tablespoons ricotta cheese mixed with half the milk to the potatoes, omit 1 tablespoon of the butter, and proceed as for Stuffed Baked Potatoes*.

Serves 4. About 165 calories each.

Steamed Spinach
Spinaci Bolliti

2½ pounds fresh or 3 packages (10 ounces each) frozen spinach
1 teaspoon salt

¼ teaspoon pepper
½ teaspoon rosemary
2 tablespoons butter or olive oil

If using fresh spinach, wash it thoroughly, changing the water several times. Remove any hard stems. Cook the fresh spinach in only the water that clings to the leaves; when limp, in about 3 minutes, drain thoroughly. If using frozen, follow the package instructions. Add the seasonings and chop, if you wish. Add the butter or oil and toss and reheat.

Serves 6. About 65 calories each.

Puréed Spinach with Garlic

Purè di Spinaci con Aglio

2 pounds or 3 bags (10 ounces each) spinach
2 tablespoons butter

1 teaspoon salt
2 cloves garlic, chopped

Wash the spinach thoroughly, remove any hard stems, and cook for a few minutes in only the water that clings to the leaves. When limp, transfer to a blender or food processor with the liquid, butter, salt, and garlic. Purée until smooth. Reheat.

If the purée is too soft, simmer, uncovered, for a minute or two. Adjust the seasoning.

Serves 6. About 65 calories each.

Simple Spinach Purée

Purè di Spinaci

2 pounds fresh or 2 packages (10 ounces each) frozen spinach
1 teaspoon salt

¼ teaspoon pepper
¼ teaspoon rosemary
a pinch basil

If using fresh spinach, wash it thoroughly, remove any hard stems, and cook in only the water that clings to the leaves. Add the remaining ingredients and cover; cook only until the spinach wilts, about 3 minutes. If using frozen, cook according to the package instructions, adding the remaining ingredients.

Purée in a blender or food processor. Taste for seasoning.

Serves 4. About 45 calories each.

Spinach with Mushrooms

Spinaci ai Funghi

2 packages (10 ounces each) frozen chopped spinach
1 cup beef broth
1 tablespoon grated onion

1 clove garlic, crushed
¼ pound mushrooms, sliced
1 teaspoon rosemary or oregano

Cook the spinach according to the package directions, substituting broth for the water and adding the onion and garlic. Stir in the mushrooms and heat for 3 minutes. Add the herb and adjust the seasoning.

Serves 4. About 55 calories each.

TOMATOES

Tomatoes, whether served as a vegetable or used in a sauce for pasta or in any Italian cookery, must be peeled. This is quite easy to do. Plunge them into boiling water for less than a minute and cool under running water; the skin can be pulled off easily. Some recipes call for seeded tomatoes. These are prepared by cutting the tomatoes in half and squeezing the seeds out. To eliminate seeds from plum tomatoes, cut a thin slice from the stem end, then squeeze. If you are using a food processor or a blender, tomatoes need not be seeded.

Grilled Tomatoes

Pomidori Grigliati

4 large tomatoes
2 tablespoons minced parsley
½ teaspoon oregano, basil, tarragon, or thyme

½ teaspoon salt
¼ teaspoon pepper
¼ teaspoon sugar

Preheat broiler.

Halve the tomatoes. Combine the remaining ingredients and mix well. Place the tomatoes on a broiler pan and spread each surface with some of the mixture. Broil for about 10 minutes, until heated through and tender.

Serves 8. About 25 calories each.

Fried Tomatoes

Pomidori Fritti

6 tomatoes, cut into ½-inch slices
2 tablespoons flour
½ teaspoon salt

½ teaspoon sugar
¼ teaspoon pepper
4 tablespoons oil or butter

Do not peel the tomatoes. Dust them with a mixture of the flour, salt, sugar, and pepper and fry in the oil or butter. Brown over high heat for about 3 minutes, turn, and brown on the other side.

Serves 6. About 90 calories each.

Stewed Tomatoes

Pomidori in Umido

¼ cup chicken broth or ¼ cup water plus 1 chicken bouillon cube
1 medium onion, chopped
½ cup chopped parsley
1 green pepper, chopped

¼ teaspoon basil
½ teaspoon salt
¼ teaspoon pepper
½ teaspoon sugar
1 can (1 pound) Italian peeled tomatoes

Combine all of the ingredients except the tomatoes in a saucepan. Simmer for 10 minutes. Add the tomatoes and simmer for 15 minutes. Adjust the seasoning.

Serves 4. About 60 calories each.

Baked Stuffed Tomatoes
Pomidori Ripieni al Forno

6 large ripe tomatoes
½ teaspoon salt
¼ teaspoon pepper
½ teaspoon nutmeg or basil
1 teaspoon sugar

1 cup chopped celery
½ cup bread crumbs
1 egg, beaten
3 teaspoons olive oil

Preheat oven to 350°.

Cut the tops off the tomatoes and remove the flesh with a spoon. Combine the remaining ingredients except the oil with the tomato flesh and juice. Refill the tomatoes. Pile the filling high and top with the oil. Bake for about 30 minutes, until the tomatoes are soft and lightly browned on top.

Serves 6. About 105 calories each.

Tomatoes Stuffed with Mushrooms
Pomidori Ripieni ai Funghi

6 large ripe tomatoes
1 onion, minced
¼ cup minced celery
2 tablespoons butter
½ pound mushrooms, sliced

1 teaspoon salt
¼ teaspoon pepper
¼ teaspoon sugar
¼ cup bread crumbs

Preheat oven to 350°.

Cut off the tops of the tomatoes, scoop out the flesh and seeds, and set aside. Sauté the onion and celery in the butter for 2 minutes; do not brown. Add the mushrooms and stir and cook for 1 minute. Season with the salt, pepper, and sugar.

Stir in the bread crumbs and enough tomato flesh and juice to make a soft mixture. Fill the tomatoes and bake for about 30 minutes.

Serves 6. About 95 calories each.

Zucchini with Tomatoes

Zucchini ai Pomidori

6 medium-large zucchini,
  sliced thin
4 medium tomatoes, peeled
  and chopped
1 clove garlic, crushed

¼ teaspoon basil or thyme
1 teaspoon salt
¼ teaspoon pepper
1½ teaspoons sugar

Combine all the ingredients in a saucepan and simmer until the zucchini are tender, about 15 minutes.

Serves 6. About 45 calories each.

Zucchini with Oil and Lemon

Zucchini all'Olio e Limone

2 pounds young zucchini
3 tablespoons olive oil
1 tablespoon water
1 teaspoon salt

½ teaspoon pepper
1 clove garlic, minced
½ to ¾ teaspoon lemon juice

Wash and cut the zucchini into thin rounds. Cook in 2 tablespoons of the oil for 1 minute; add the remaining ingredients except the lemon juice. Simmer for less than 10 minutes; the zucchini should be crisp-tender. Add the lemon juice mixed with the remaining oil and serve at once.

Serves 4. About 115 calories each.

Baked Zucchini

Zucchini alla Romana

2 large onions, minced
2 tablespoons olive oil
½ cup diced celery
2 pounds young zucchini, sliced
1 teaspoon salt
¼ teaspoon pepper

½ teaspoon oregano
1 clove garlic, crushed
¼ cup seasoned Italian bread crumbs
3 tablespoons grated Parmesan cheese (optional)

Preheat oven to 350°.

Sauté the onions in the oil for 2 minutes in a baking dish. Add the celery and cook until both are softened; do not brown. Add the zucchini and seasonings, stir, and cook for about 5 minutes. Top with the crumbs and the cheese, if you wish, and bake for 15 minutes.

Serves 6. About 85 calories each without cheese; about 125 calories each with cheese.

Zucchini with Onions

Zucchini ai Cipolline

2 large onions, chopped fine
1 clove garlic, crushed
¼ cup chicken or beef broth
6 medium zucchini, sliced
3 medium tomatoes, peeled and chopped

½ teaspoon oregano
1 teaspoon salt
¼ teaspoon pepper
pinch sugar

Brown the onion and garlic in the broth in a nonstick pan, turning to brown evenly. This should take no more than 5 minutes. Add the zucchini and brown, turning carefully to brown evenly, about 5 minutes. Add the remaining ingredients, cover, and simmer for 10 minutes, until the zucchini are tender. Stir several times.

Serves 6. About 50 calories each.

Fried Zucchini

Zucchini Fritti

6 medium zucchini, about 2
  pounds
2 tablespoons flour
1 teaspoon salt

¼ teaspoon pepper
1 clove garlic, crushed
3 tablespoons olive oil

Wash and cut the zucchini into rounds ¼ inch thick; trim the ends if necessary. Coat with a mixture of the flour, salt, pepper, and garlic and fry in the oil until golden. Drain on paper toweling.

    Serves 6. About 85 calories each.

Salad

IN ITALY, A FAVORITE salad is *insalata mista,* mixed greens, delicate and delicious. Sometimes the greens are combined with tomatoes, onions, cucumbers, peppers, and fennel. These salads accompany or follow the main course. Vegetable salads, such as asparagus or string beans, are often served first, while salads containing bits of meat, fish, or poultry may be included in the antipasto.

Salad greens should be washed gently in cold water and dried thoroughly, then pulled apart and torn (with the exception of Belgian endive) into bite-size pieces. The greens should be young and crisp and the herbs fresh, if possible, for there is a real difference between fresh and dried herbs, particularly in salads. Use a large bowl; you cannot toss salad properly in a small one. Preferably, the dressing should be added and the salad tossed at the last minute, but if the dressing must be added earlier, at least postpone the tossing for as long as possible.

Italians do not customarily serve heavy dressings such as mayonnaise, preferring the French type — oil, vinegar, salt, pepper, and a whiff (or more) of garlic. This is of course a help to the low-calorie fans. A small quantity is sufficient to "dress" a well-tossed salad. The Romans ate their salad with nothing on it but salt; in fact, the word itself comes from the Latin (and Italian) *sal,* which means salt. It's nice that we can improve on bare salt without adding too many calories.

Mixed Green Salad I

Insalata Mista I

1 head lettuce	1 teaspoon salt
½ head curly endive	¼ teaspoon pepper
½ head romaine	½ teaspoon herbs: tarragon,
2½ to 3 tablespoons olive oil	basil, or oregano (optional)
2 tablespoons wine vinegar	½ clove garlic (optional)

Wash the greens. Break the lettuce and endive; cut the romaine into 1-inch pieces. Dry and place in a towel in the refrigerator until ready to put the salad together.

Put the greens into a large salad bowl, preferably of wood. Combine the remaining ingredients in a jar and shake well. Pour over the salad a few minutes before serving. Toss.

Serves 6. About 60 to 70 calories each.

Variations

Mixed Green Salad II

Insalata Mista II

Substitute 1 small head escarole, 1 small head iceberg lettuce, and ½ bunch watercress or ¼ pound spinach for the greens and proceed as for Mixed Green Salad I*, pulling off the heavy stems from the watercress.

Serves 6. About 60 to 70 calories each.

Lettuce and Rugula Salad

Insalata di Lattuga e la Rughetta

Substitute 1 large head Boston lettuce and 1 bunch of rugula (sometimes called arugula or rocket) for the greens and proceed as for Mixed Green Salad I*.

Serves 6. About 60 to 70 calories each.

Mixed Green Salad III

Insalata Mista III

2 heads Bibb or Boston lettuce
½ head curly chicory or
    escarole
1 bunch rugula, field salad, or
    leaf lettuce
2 carrots, scraped and
    shredded
1 green pepper, slivered
3 stalks celery, scraped and
    slivered

1 fennel bulb, slivered
3 small tomatoes, peeled and
    cut in slices and wedges
Dressing: 2 to 3 tablespoons
    oil
1 tablespoon vinegar
1 teaspoon prepared mustard
1 teaspoon salt
¼ teaspoon pepper

Wash the lettuce in very cold water and break into bite-size pieces. If any of the ingredients are not available or not really fresh, omit them. Make substitutions such as: cucumber for carrots or pepper; other greens for the ones suggested, such as romaine or even iceberg. Place all of the salad in a large bowl. Add the tomatoes last so they don't fall apart.

Combine the oil, vinegar, mustard, salt, and pepper and shake well. Pour over the salad a few minutes before serving and toss gently.

Serves 6. About 75 calories each.

Green Salad with Salami

Insalata Verde al Salame

½ head iceberg lettuce
1 head soft lettuce
½ head curly endive or
    escarole

4 slices salami, cut into thin
    strips
¼ cup Low-Calorie Italian-
    Type Dressing*

Wash and dry the greens and tear them into bite-size pieces. Place in a salad bowl with the salami and toss with the dressing.

Serves 6. About 75 calories each.

Lettuce Salad

Insalata di Lattuga

1 large or 2 medium heads
   lettuce
2½ tablespoons olive oil
1½ to 2 tablespoons wine
   vinegar
¾ to 1 teaspoon salt

¼ teaspoon pepper
1 clove garlic, cut in half and
   slightly crushed (optional)

Wash the lettuce, pull it apart, and spread to dry on paper toweling or shake in a lettuce basket. Remove any wilted leaves and tear the rest into 1-inch pieces. Place in a bowl. Chill.

Combine the remaining ingredients and shake well. Remove the garlic, if used, and pour dressing over the greens about 5 minutes before serving. Toss. You may rub the bowl with garlic instead of putting it in the dressing if you prefer.

Serves 6. About 60 calories each.

Variations

Dandelion Salad

Insalata di Cicoria

Substitute 1 pound of dandelion greens for the lettuce and proceed as for Lettuce Salad*.

Serves 6. About 60 calories each.

Garden Lettuce Salad

Insalata da Taglio

Substitute about 1 pound of leaf lettuce for the head lettuce, omit the garlic, and proceed as for Lettuce Salad*.

Serves 6. About 60 calories each.

Romaine Salad

Insalata di Lattuga Romana

1 large head romaine
1 large Bermuda onion, sliced
  thin
2 tablespoons oil
2 tablespoons wine vinegar

1 teaspoon salt
¼ teaspoon pepper
½ teaspoon oregano (optional)

Pull the romaine apart into bite-size pieces, discarding any damaged outside leaves. Place in a salad bowl with the onion rings.

Combine the remaining ingredients. Pour over the salad 5 to 10 minutes before serving and toss at the last minute.

Serves 6. About 35 calories each.

Chef Salad Julienne

Insalata alla Buongustaia

1 tomato, peeled and chopped
1 cucumber, peeled and
  slivered
2 stalks celery, scraped and
  slivered
2 carrots, scraped and slivered
1 green pepper, seeded and
  slivered
1 onion, slivered
3 scallions, slivered

1 cup thin-cut cooked green
  beans
1 cup cooked chicken, slivered
½ cup thin strips Swiss cheese
2 cups soft lettuce, broken into
  bite-size pieces
2 tablespoons olive oil
2 tablespoons vinegar
1 teaspoon salt
¼ teaspoon pepper

Combine all but the last four ingredients in a salad bowl. Mix the oil and vinegar with the salt and pepper. Pour over the salad about 5 minutes before serving and toss at the table.

Serves 6. About 175 calories each.

Tomato Salad I

Insalata di Pomidori con Olio I

4 ripe tomatoes, peeled
3 scallions, chopped
1 teaspoon salt
¼ teaspoon pepper
½ teaspoon sugar

½ teaspoon thyme
1 clove garlic, crushed
2 tablespoons olive oil
1 tablespoon lemon juice

Halve the tomatoes and squeeze out some of the seeds. Slice the flesh. Combine with the scallions.

Combine the remaining ingredients, mix, and pour over the tomatoes. Let stand for 15 to 20 minutes before serving.

Serves 6. About 55 calories each.

Tomato Salad II

Insalata di Pomidori con Olio II

4 large or 6 medium tomatoes,
  peeled
4 scallions or 3 shallots,
  chopped
½ teaspoon salt

½ teaspoon sugar
¼ teaspoon pepper
1 tablespoon thyme or oregano
2 tablespoons olive oil

Cut the tomatoes into thin slices and place on a platter so they will lie flat. Sprinkle with the remaining ingredients except the oil. Dribble the oil over and let stand at least 4 hours in the refrigerator.

Serves 6. About 50 calories each.

Raw Vegetable Salad

Insalata di Verdure I

1 green pepper, cut into strips
1 large carrot, cut into strips
2 stalks celery, cut into strips
1 small cucumber, diced
1 pimiento, diced

6 radishes, diced
2 cups shredded cabbage
⅓ cup Special* or Mustard
  Dressing*

Combine all of the ingredients except the dressing in a large salad bowl. Pour over ¼ cup of the dressing and toss. If the vegetables are not coated enough, add the remaining dressing and toss again. Let stand about 30 minutes.

Serves 6. About 40 calories each.

Mixed Vegetable Salad

Insalata di Verdure II

2 cups cooked green beans
1 cup cooked fava beans
2 large tomatoes, peeled and cut into pieces
6 scallions, coarsely chopped
2 medium potatoes, cooked, peeled, and diced or sliced thin
3 tablespoons oil

3 tablespoons vinegar
1 teaspoon salt
¼ teaspoon pepper
pinch sugar
1 teaspoon dried or 1 tablespoon fresh chopped basil
2 tablespoons minced parsley (garnish)

Put the vegetables into a salad bowl, arranging them attractively. Combine the remaining ingredients except the parsley and blend well. Pour the dressing over the vegetables, toss, and top with the parsley.

Serves 6. About 60 calories each.

Cucumber Salad

Insalata di Cetrioli

3 large cucumbers, peeled
salt
⅓ cup vinegar

2 tablespoons sugar
½ teaspoon pepper
2 tablespoons olive oil (optional)

Slice the cucumbers very thin and layer them in a bowl alternately with the salt. Weight down and let stand several hours or overnight.

Wash in a sieve or colander under running cold water. Drain and dress with a mixture of the vinegar, sugar, and pepper. Add the oil, if you wish.

Serves 6. About 20 calories each; 45 calories with oil.

Green Bean Salad

Insalata di Fagiolini

1 pound green beans	½ teaspoon salt
2 tablespoons olive oil	¼ teaspoon pepper
1 tablespoon wine vinegar	1 clove garlic, crushed

Cut off the ends and cook the beans in salted water to cover for 15 to 20 minutes, until just tender. Drain and cool. Combine the remaining ingredients and mix thoroughly.

Place the beans in a shallow bowl in a row all going in one direction. Pour the dressing over and let stand for 30 minutes. Chill, if you wish.

Serves 6. About 55 calories each.

Shredded Carrot Salad

Insalata di Carote

8 medium to large carrots	1 teaspoon salt
3 tablespoons olive oil	¼ teaspoon sugar
1 tablespoon lemon juice	1 tablespoon minced parsley

Scrape the carrots and shred, using the grating blade of a food processor, or grate them on the largest holes of a hand grater. Add the remaining ingredients. Toss and adjust the seasoning to taste

Serves 6. About 100 calories each.

Raw Mushroom Salad

Insalata di Funghi Crudi

The mushrooms must be white and fresh to serve raw.

1 pound mushrooms	½ teaspoon salt
¼ cup oil	¼ teaspoon pepper
1 tablespoon vinegar	¼ teaspoon oregano
1 tablespoon lemon juice	soft salad greens

Wipe the mushrooms and cut off or pull out the stems and discard. Slice the mushroom caps thin. Mix the oil, vinegar, lemon juice, salt, pepper, and oregano and pour over the mushrooms. Toss gently but thoroughly. Let stand in the refrigerator for about 1 hour. Serve on salad greens.

Serves 6. About 100 calories each.

Asparagus Salad

Insalata di Asparagi

2½ to 3 pounds asparagus	1 teaspoon salt
3 tablespoons oil	¼ teaspoon pepper
2 tablespoons wine vinegar	

Cut off the ends of the asparagus, making the spears all the same length. Scrape the stalks about halfway up. Tie the spears in bunches and place in a steamer or put the ends in water. Cover tight and boil the water so that the tops steam while the ends boil. Cook until tender, about 15 to 20 minutes. Don't overcook; asparagus must not be mushy. Remove to a platter and let cool. Drain the liquid from the platter. Spread out the asparagus and chill it while you make the dressing.

Combine the oil, vinegar, salt, and pepper, blend well, and pour over the asparagus.

Serves 6. About 90 calories each.

Fennel Salad I

Insalata di Finocchio I

2 bulbs fennel	1 clove garlic, crushed
3 tablespoons olive oil	½ teaspoon salt
1 tablespoon vinegar	¼ teaspoon pepper

Wash the fennel and trim off the stem and any outer tough leaves. Slice as thin as possible and put into ice water to crisp. Dry thoroughly and put into a chilled bowl.

Add a mixture of the oil, vinegar, garlic, salt, and pepper and toss.

Serves 4. About 100 calories each.

Fennel Salad II

Insalata di Finocchio II

1 pound fennel	2 tablespoons wine vinegar
1 small head iceberg lettuce	½ teaspoon salt
1 clove garlic, crushed	¼ teaspoon pepper
3 tablespoons oil	

Dice the fennel, removing the stems and any discolored leaves. Pull the lettuce into small bite-size pieces. Combine the remaining ingredients and pour over the fennel and lettuce. Toss thoroughly. Let stand for 30 minutes.

Serves 8. About 55 calories each.

Fennel Salad with Cucumber

Insalata di Finocchio III

2 bulbs fennel	2 teaspoons lemon juice
1 large cucumber, peeled and diced	½ teaspoon salt
6 radishes, sliced	¼ teaspoon pepper
2 tablespoons olive oil	1 clove garlic

Cut the fennel into thin strips, discarding any tough outside stalks. Combine with the cucumber and radishes. Combine the oil, lemon juice, salt, pepper, and garlic and toss with the vegetables.

Serves 4. About 70 calories each.

Cooked Fennel Salad

Insalata di Finocchio IV

4 large bulbs fennel salad greens
¼ cup salad dressing

Remove the outer tough leaves of the fennel and cut the bulbs in half. Boil in very lightly salted water to cover until tender but not mushy, about 12 minutes. Drain and chill. Serve with Special Dressing* or Low-Calorie Italian-Type Dressing* on soft salad greens.

Serves 8. About 80 calories each with Low-Calorie Italian Dressing*, about 35 calories each with Special* or Tomato Dressing*.

Coleslaw

Insalata di Cavolo Bianco

4 cups shredded cabbage ⅓ cup wine vinegar
¼ cup chopped parsley ½ cup skim-milk yogurt
½ cup slivered carrots 1 teaspoon salt
¼ cup finely chopped green ¼ teaspoon sugar
  pepper

Mix the vegetables in a bowl. Combine the vinegar, yogurt, salt, and sugar; blend thoroughly and pour over the vegetables. Mix well.

Serves 6. About 45 calories each.

Potato Salad I

Insalata di Patate I

6 medium potatoes 1 teaspoon salt
1 medium onion, sliced thin ¼ teaspoon pepper
3 tablespoons olive oil 2 tablespoons minced parsley
1½ tablespoons wine vinegar

Boil the potatoes in their jackets until soft. Peel and slice thin. Layer in a bowl with the onion. Combine the remaining ingredients, mix well, and pour over. If you work quickly, you can pour the dressing over while the potatoes are still warm, which improves the salad. Chill.
    Serves 6. About 125 calories each.

Potato Salad II

Insalata di Patate II

1½ pounds potatoes, boiled in
    their jackets
1 stalk celery, diced
2 small onions, diced
2 small pickles, chopped
1 tablespoon chopped fresh or
    1 teaspoon dried basil

1 teaspoon salt
¼ teaspoon pepper
3 tablespoons oil
1 tablespoon vinegar
4 anchovy fillets, chopped
1 tablespoon capers (optional)

Peel the potatoes as soon as they are cool enough to handle. Dice them and combine with the celery, onions, pickles, and basil. Mix the salt, pepper, oil, and vinegar together. Add the anchovies and capers, if you wish, to the dressing. Pour over the salad and toss gently.
    Serves 6. About 140 calories each.

Orange Salad

Insalata di Aranci

6 medium oranges
1 large red or Bermuda onion,
    sliced thin
¼ pound Swiss cheese, sliced

2 tablespoons Vinaigrette
    Dressing*
1 teaspoon sugar

Peel the oranges with a sharp knife, cutting off all of the white fibers. Save a little of the juice. Section or slice the oranges. Separate the onion into rings. Mix the oranges, onion, and the cheese. Mix the dressing with 1 tablespoon of orange juice and the sugar and pour over.

Serves 6. About 125 calories each.

Shrimp Salad I

Insalata di Scampi II

2 pounds medium or small raw shrimp
1 large head Boston lettuce
1 bunch watercress
2 scallions, minced
2 tablespoons salad oil
2 tablespoons vinegar
1 pound cottage cheese

Cook the shrimp in water barely to cover for about 3 minutes, until they turn pink. Cool, peel, and devein. If they are a good size, cut them in half lengthwise.

Meanwhile, wash and tear up the lettuce. Wash the watercress thoroughly, remove the tough stems, and cut up about half of the cress. Combine the lettuce, cut-up cress, and scallions in a salad bowl and add the mixed oil and vinegar; toss.

When the shrimp are cold, add to the lettuce with the cottage cheese and toss all together. Garnish with the remaining watercress around the edge of the bowl. Chill until ready to serve.

Serves 6. About 180 calories each.

Tuna Salad with Egg

Insalata di Tonno con Uova

1 can (7 ounces) tuna packed in water, flaked
2 tablespoons minced parsley
2 cups shredded lettuce
2 tablespoons olive oil
1 tablespoon lemon juice
1 teaspoon salt
¼ teaspoon pepper
2 hard-cooked eggs, coarsely chopped

Combine all the ingredients except the eggs and toss thoroughly. Add the eggs and toss gently.

Serves 4. About 120 calories each.

SALAD DRESSINGS

Olive oil has far more flavor than other salad oils; it is especially important to choose it when one wishes to cut down on quantity in order to save calories. Similarly, be sure to use wine vinegar (add garlic or herbs yourself), as it not only tastes better than cider vinegar, but, being less "sour," requires less oil to make the dressing palatable. You can't cut down on the oil in a recipe but you can use a minimum of dressing.

Low-Calorie Italian-Type Dressing
Condimento al' Tipo Italiano

2 tablespoons olive oil
½ cup buttermilk
¼ cup wine vinegar
1 clove garlic, crushed or cut
   in half

1 teaspoon salt
¼ teaspoon pepper
⅛ teaspoon oregano or
   tarragon (optional)

Combine all the ingredients. Put into a jar and refrigerate for several hours. Shake thoroughly. If using cut garlic, remove it. Be sure to shake before serving or purée in a blender for a few seconds.

About ¾ cup. About 60 calories per tablespoon.

Italian Dressing
Condimento all'Italiana

½ cup olive oil
¼ cup wine vinegar
1 clove garlic, crushed or cut

½ teaspoon salt
¼ teaspoon pepper
⅛ teaspoon oregano

Combine all of the ingredients. Mix thoroughly and let stand for several hours. If using the cut garlic, remove before serving. Shake well before serving.

About ¾ cup. About 80 calories per tablespoon.

Vinaigrette Dressing

Salsa Vinaigrette

½ cup red wine vinegar   1 teaspoon salt
½ cup olive oil   ¼ teaspoon pepper

Combine all the ingredients and stir thoroughly or shake in a jar.

About 1 cup. About 65 calories per tablespoon.

Tomato Dressing

Condimento al Pomidoro

3 tablespoons low-calorie   1 teaspoon basil
   cottage cheese or ricotta   ½ teaspoon thyme
1 cup tomato juice   1 teaspoon salt
2 tablespoons wine vinegar   ¼ teaspoon pepper
1 large clove garlic, crushed   ¼ teaspoon sugar

Smooth the cheese and then blend it with the tomato juice. Stir in the remaining ingredients.

About 1¼ cups. About 12 calories per tablespoon.

Citrus Dressing I

Condimento di Frutta I

¼ cup lemon juice   ½ teaspoon salt
¾ cup orange juice   1 tablespoon sugar

Shake all the ingredients together.

About 1 cup. About 10 calories per tablespoon.

Citrus Dressing II

Condimento di Frutta II

⅓ cup orange juice and ⅓ cup
  pineapple juice or ⅔ cup of
  either
3 tablespoons lemon juice

½ teaspoon salt
1 tablespoon sugar
1 egg yolk
3 tablespoons milk

Combine the ingredients except the egg and milk. Beat the egg yolk with the milk and add to the rest of the dressing. Mix again. It is a good idea to shake the dressing in a jar.

About 1¼ cups. About 20 calories per tablespoon.

Ricotta Dressing

Condimento alla Ricotta

6 tablespoons ricotta cheese
2 tablespoons sour cream
1 tablespoon lemon juice

¼ teaspoon salt
1 teaspoon sugar

Smooth the cheese with the sour cream and lemon juice. Add the salt and sugar.

About ½ cup. About 25 calories per tablespoon.

Special Dressing

Condimento Speziale

1 cup yogurt
1 hard-cooked egg, chopped or
  grated
¼ cup chili sauce or catsup

2 tablespoons minced
  scallions
1 teaspoon lemon juice
¼ teaspoon basil

Combine all the ingredients. Mix thoroughly. Cover and refrigerate for several hours.

About 1¼ cups. About 15 calories per tablespoon.

Mustard Dressing

Condimento di Senape

1 tablespoon butter
2 tablespoons flour
1 cup skim milk
2 tablespoons prepared
  mustard

1 teaspoon salt
¼ teaspoon pepper
2 teaspoons sugar
2 tablespoons vinegar

Melt the butter, blend in the flour, and stir in the milk slowly. Cook while stirring until thickened. Add the mustard, salt, pepper, and sugar, and stir in the vinegar gradually. Chill for several hours.

About 1¼ cups. About 20 calories per tablespoon.

Cooked Dressing

Condimento Bollito

1 tablespoon sugar
2 tablespoons flour
1 teaspoon dry mustard
1 teaspoon salt
¼ teaspoon pepper

¼ cup water
½ cup skim milk
1 egg, beaten
3 tablespoons lemon juice or 2
  tablespoons white vinegar

Mix the dry ingredients with the water in a double boiler. Heat and stir in the skim milk. Add the egg while stirring, then the lemon juice or vinegar. Adjust the seasoning and cook until thickened. Chill.

About 1 cup. About 25 calories per tablespoon.

Desserts

FRUIT

Fresh fruit is served at almost every Italian meal, and no wonder, for it is plentiful and reasonable, and the colorful displays in the markets are almost irresistible. A bowl on the table can double as a handsome centerpiece.

Raw fruit is frequently accompanied by a piece of cheese; a low-calorie cheese such as ricotta is more than acceptable. Combinations of fresh fruits in a *macedonia* give the cook an opportunity to use any variety and what the seasons have to offer. Certainly, fruit does not have to be served unadorned; a little dressing of orange or lemon juice or a sprinkle of sugar, wine, or a sweet liqueur will work wonders. Nor need fruit be served raw; ending a meal with poached, broiled, baked, or stuffed fruit is also a delight. Fruit is not only a low-calorie ending, but, according to Italians, it is the best dessert there is.

The calories of different fruits vary considerably; here are approximate figures. Whole fruit is estimated according to one of medium size.

Apple 85
Apricots (3) 50
Banana 130
Blueberries (1 cup) 85
Cantaloupe (half) 50
Cherries (15) 50
Figs (2) 70
Grapefruit (half) 40
Grapes (¼ pound) 70
Honeydew melon (quarter) 35

Nectarine 30
Orange 65
Peach 45
Pear 80
Pineapple (1¾ inch slice) 40
Plums (2) 50
Raspberries (½ cup) 40
Strawberries (½ cup) 30
Watermelon (1 small slice) 40

Mixed Fresh Fruit

Macedonia di Frutta

½ cup orange juice
1 tablespoon lemon juice
2 apples
2 pears
3 peaches
1 large banana
3 tablespoons sugar
3 tablespoons maraschino
  liqueur, kirsch, or other fruit
  liqueur

other fruit such as: ½ pound
  white seedless grapes, 1 cup
  fresh strawberries, 1 cup
  cherries, 2 nectarines, 4
  plums

Put the orange and lemon juice into a serving bowl. Peel and core the apples and pears and cut into ¼- to ½-inch cubes. Put into the fruit juices. Peel and pit the peaches, dice, and add to the fruit with the sliced banana. Sprinkle with the sugar and add the liqueur. Toss gently and refrigerate for several hours.

Turn once or twice to insure that all the pieces are coated with liquid, otherwise they will darken. Add or substitute any other fruit in season if you wish.

Serves 6. About 140 calories each without extra fruit.

Fresh Fruit in a Melon

Melone Ripieno

1 ripe cantaloupe or 1 small
  honeydew melon
2 large peaches
2 pears

juice of ½ lemon
1 pint fresh strawberries
⅓ sup sugar
¼ cup red wine

Cut the cantaloupe in half and scoop out the flesh with a melon-ball cutter or cut it into ½-inch cubes; reserve. Scrape out the shells and put them in the freezer while you prepare the remaining fruit.

Peel and pit the peaches; peel and core the pears. Cut

the flesh into ½-inch cubes. Place in a bowl and sprinkle
with the lemon juice at once.

Hull the berries and add them and the melon balls to
the other fruit. Sprinkle with the sugar and the wine.
Toss and fill the cantaloupe shells with fruit.

Serves 6. About 130 calories each.

Strawberries and Melon with Banana Cream Sauce

Fragole e Melone con Banane

2 pints strawberries
½ cup yogurt
2 tablespoons sugar

2 small ripe bananas
2 cups melon balls

Wash and then hull the berries, cut into pieces, and set
aside. Combine the yogurt and sugar. Mash the bananas with a fork and stir into the yogurt. Combine the
melon balls and strawberries; put half in a large serving
bowl, preferably glass. Spoon over half the banana mixture, add the remaining fruit, and spoon over the rest of
the sauce. Garnish, if you wish, with a few whole berries.

Serves 6. About 110 calories each.

Strawberries with Liqueur

Fragole al Rosolio

1 quart strawberries
2 tablespoons sugar

4 tablespoons Curaçao,
  Cointreau, or any fruit
  liqueur

Wash the berries and hull them. Place in a serving bowl,
preferably glass. Combine the sugar with the liqueur
and pour over the berries. Toss gently two or three times
before serving either chilled or at room temperature.

Serves 4. About 150 calories each.

Strawberries in Red Wine

Fragole al Vino Rosso

2 pints strawberries   1 cup red wine
⅓ cup sugar

Wash and hull the strawberries. Put into a serving bowl, preferably glass, and toss gently with the sugar. Add the wine and let stand in the refrigerator for a couple of hours, tossing gently a few times.
Serves 4. About 120 calories each.

Strawberries with White Wine

Fragole al Vino Bianco

2 pints strawberries   ⅔ cup white wine
3 tablespoons sugar   grated rind of 1 orange

Wash and then hull the berries and sprinkle with the sugar. Pour the wine over and sprinkle with the orange rind. Refrigerate for several hours.
Serves 4. About 110 calories each.

Ruby Strawberries

Fragole con Salsa di Lamponi

2 pints strawberries   2 tablespoons sugar
1 package (1 pound) frozen   1 teaspoon lemon juice or 1
  raspberries   tablespoon brandy

Wash and then hull the berries and put into a serving bowl, preferably glass. Chill in the refrigerator.
To make the sauce, thaw the raspberries and purée in a blender with the sugar and lemon juice or brandy. Strain, pushing through all the juice you can. Pour over the berries a few minutes before serving.
Serves 4. About 110 calories each.

Poached Pears with Strawberries

Pere con Fragole

4 firm pears
1 cup water
2 tablespoons sugar

1 package (1 pound) frozen
   sliced strawberries

Peel and poach the pears, uncovered, in the water and sugar. When soft, let cool. Add the thawed strawberries and stir gently.

Serves 4. About 160 calories each.

Baked Pears Stuffed with Ricotta Cheese

Pere Ripiene con Ricotta

2 large or 4 small pears
¼ teaspoon grated nutmeg
⅛ teaspoon allspice
1 cup water

1 teaspoon vanilla
¼ cup ricotta cheese
1 tablespoon sugar
2 tablespoons buttermilk

Preheat oven to 250°.

Peel the pears, cut them in half, and core them. Rub them with the nutmeg and allspice. Put into a pan with the water and vanilla. Bake until softened, basting several times.

Mix the cheese with the sugar and buttermilk and fill the pears. Serve warm or cold.

Serves 4. About 75 calories each.

Stewed Pears

Pere in Composta

3 large or 6 small pears
juice of ½ lemon
½ cup sugar

1 2-inch piece cinnamon or ½
   teaspoon ground cinnamon

Peel the pears, cut in halves or quarters, and core them. Put into water to cover with the lemon juice. Pour off most of the water into a pot, heat, add the sugar and cinnamon, and boil for 2 minutes. Put in the pears and remaining water. Cook until soft but not mushy. Remove, with a slotted spoon, to a serving dish. Boil the liquid to reduce it and pour over the pears. Serve warm or chilled.

Serves 4. About 175 calories each.

Stewed Peaches

Pesche in Composta

6 large peaches
1 tablespoon lemon juice
2 cups water

½ cup sugar
½ cup red wine, sherry, or
rum

Peel the peaches and sprinkle with the lemon juice. Bring the water to a boil with the sugar and liquor. Simmer, uncovered, for 10 minutes.

Add the peaches and simmer for 10 to 12 minutes, until they are soft. Turn the fruit several times. Remove the peaches with the liquid to a serving bowl and let stand in refrigerator for an hour or more before serving.

Serves 6. About 120 calories each.

Peaches in Brandy-Orange Sauce

Pesche alla Grappa e Aranci

6 large peaches
1½ ounces brandy or Strega
2 tablespoons sugar

¼ cup orange juice
1 teaspoon grated orange rind

Plunge the peaches into boiling water for a minute to facilitate peeling. Peel and slice them. Combine the remaining ingredients and pour over the peaches. Cover and let stand in the refrigerator for at least 2 hours.

Serves 6. About 100 calories each.

Peaches with Raspberries

Pesche con Lamponi

1 can (1 pound) peach halves
  packed in water
1 package (10 ounces) frozen
  raspberries

1 tablespoon rum or sweet
  sherry

Drain the peaches, reserving the liquid. Purée the raspberries in a blender with the rum or sherry and ½ cup of the peach juice. Strain.

Place peaches open side up in a spoonful of sauce in a low serving bowl or individual glass serving dishes. Fill the hollow in each peach with sauce.

Serves 4. About 140 calories each.

Peaches in Aspic

Pesche in Gelatina

1 can (1 pound) peaches
  packed in water
2 envelopes unflavored gelatin
¼ cup cold water

1½ cups skim milk
¼ cup sugar
1 tablespoon brandy or rum

Drain the peaches and dice, reserving the liquid, and set aside. Heat the liquid and boil to reduce to ½ cup. Soften the gelatin in the water, add the milk, fruit juice, and sugar. Heat and stir only until the gelatin is dissolved. Add the brandy or rum.

Purée in a blender or food processor with half the peaches. When smooth, add to the remaining peaches, mix, and pour into a slightly greased mold. Chill until firm. Turn out to serve.

Serves 6. About 85 calories each.

Melon Balls in Wine

Melone al Vino Bianco

1 large cantaloupe or
  honeydew melon
1 envelope diet lime gelatin
1 tablespoon lime or lemon
  juice

½ cup boiling water
1 tablespoon sugar
1 cup white wine

Cut balls from the melon and set aside. Save any juice and squeeze the liquid from the shells. Add the lime or lemon juice and soften the gelatin in this. Pour the boiling water over and stir until the gelatin is dissolved. Add the sugar and wine and chill until syrupy. Stir in the melon balls in a serving dish or 6 individual sherbet glasses. Chill again.

Serves 4. About 95 calories each.

Baked Apples

Mele Cotte

4 apples
¼ cup raisins, plumped

¼ cup sugar
½ cup white wine

Preheat oven to 350°.

Core the apples and peel around the top for about ¾ inch. Place the apples in a baking dish. Put a few raisins in each hole. Add 1 teaspoon of the sugar and the remaining raisins. Sprinkle the remaining sugar over the top. Pour the wine over and bake for about 30 minutes, until the apples are soft. Baste several times and serve the apples with the juice spooned over.

Serves 4. About 120 calories each.

Baked Bananas I

Banane Cotte

2 tablespoons melted butter
3 tablespoons sugar

1 tablespoon rum
4 small bananas

Preheat oven to 300°.

Combine the butter, sugar, and rum and heat until the sugar is dissolved. Put the bananas into the pan, either whole or halved lengthwise. Bake, turning once or twice, for 15 minutes. Put the bananas on a serving plate or 4 individual plates and spoon the sauce over. Serve chilled, at room temperature, or warm.

Serves 4. About 185 calories each.

Baked Bananas II

Banane al Forno

6 large ripe bananas
2 tablespoons melted
  mayonnaise or butter
¼ cup sugar

1 teaspoon cinnamon
whipped skim milk (see page
  267) or low-calorie
  whipped topping (optional)

Preheat oven to 350°.

Peel the bananas and place in a shallow baking dish. Brush with the mayonnaise or butter and sprinkle with the sugar and cinnamon. Bake for 20 minutes.

Serves 6. About 200 calories each.

Broiled Sherried Grapefruit

Pompelmo alla Griglia

2 grapefruits
about 2 tablespoons brown
  sugar

4 teaspoons sherry

Preheat broiler.

Cut the grapefruits in half and loosen the sections.

Sprinkle with the sugar. The amount will depend upon how sweet the grapefruit is; usually 1 teaspoon per half is about right. Pour 1 teaspoon sherry over each and broil until golden on top. Do not put too close to the heat or the sugar will burn.

Serves 4. About 65 calories each.

PUDDINGS

Puddings, *budini,* can be made to fit the menus of the calorie-conscious if they are carefully chosen. There are a number of tasty Italian-American ones here.

Zabaglione is a famous and perhaps the favorite dessert of Italy, a delicious combination of eggs, sugar, and wine, preferably Marsala. It must be made with care. It should never be cooked over direct heat; the most effective way to present it is to cook it at the table in a chafing dish or double boiler. If prepared in the kitchen, it must be cooked gently over simmering water and presented with pride. It may be served hot, warm, or cold.

Italian Custard

Zabaglione

6 egg yolks   6 tablespoons Marsala
6 tablespoons fine sugar

Beat the egg yolks with a rotary beater in the top of a double boiler or whatever utensil you are going to cook in. Beat in the sugar and continue to beat until pale and fluffy. Put over boiling water and beat in the Marsala. Continue to beat and cook until it is thickened, about 6 minutes. Do not allow the custard to boil. Remove from the heat and beat for ½ minute. Serve warm or cold in dessert glasses.

Serves 6. About 175 calories each.

Baked Custard

Crema

2 eggs
2 tablespoons sugar
2 cups skim milk

1 teaspoon vanilla or ½
    teaspoon almond extract

Preheat oven to 325°.
Beat the eggs lightly with the sugar. Add the milk slowly and then the flavoring. Stir and pour into 4 custard cups. Put the cups in a hot water bath, with the water coming to about 1 inch from the top of the cups. Bake for about 1 hour. Cool.
Serves 4. About 100 calories each.

Coffee Custard

Crema al Caffè

5 egg yolks
2½ cups skim milk

⅓ cup sugar
3 tablespoons instant coffee

Preheat oven to 325°.
Beat the egg yolks. Scald the milk with the sugar and coffee. Add the eggs slowly while stirring. Pour into 6 custard cups or a serving dish and bake in a hot water bath for about 50 minutes.
Serves 6. About 160 calories each.

Spanish Cream

Crema Espagnola

½ cup sugar
1 envelope unflavored gelatin
1 cup milk

1½ cups skim milk
3 eggs, separated
1 teaspoon vanilla or brandy

Combine the sugar and gelatin and stir in both milks slowly. Heat until the gelatin and sugar are dissolved.

Beat the egg yolks; stir in a little of the milk mixture. Return all to the pan and cook and stir until thickened.

Beat the egg whites and fold into the warm mixture. Add the vanilla or brandy. Pour into a serving bowl, preferably clear glass. Chill.

The opaque custard will be on top and a clear jelly on the bottom, which shows well in a glass serving dish. This dessert can also be turned out on a serving plate.

Serves 6. About 170 calories each.

Rice Pudding

Budino di Riso

½ cup rice
3 cups skim milk
½ cup sugar

1 teaspoon vanilla and/or ½
   teaspoon nutmeg

Preheat oven to 325°.

Put the rice in a buttered 6-cup baking dish. Add the milk, sugar, and vanilla or nutmeg. Bake for 2 hours, stirring several times during the first 1½ hours.

Let it rest for the last half-hour of cooking so the top will be lightly browned. Serve warm or at room temperature.

Serves 6. About 175 calories each.

Cold Rice Pudding

Budino di Riso Freddo

1 cup water
2 cups skim milk
½ cup rice
6 tablespoons sugar

1 teaspoon vanilla
½ teaspoon almond extract
1 cup ricotta, beaten

Put the water, milk, and rice into a double boiler, cover, and cook for 1 hour, stirring several times. Uncover and continue to cook until thick, about ½ hour. Stir in the sugar, vanilla, and almond extract. Chill.

Fold in the ricotta. Serve in individual dishes or a serving bowl, preferably glass.

Serves 6. About 160 calories each.

Bread Pudding

Budino di Pane

4 slices stale bread, lightly
  buttered
2 tablespoons raisins
½ teaspoon cinnamon

½ teaspoon grated lemon rind
3 eggs
½ cup sugar
2½ cups skim milk

Preheat oven to 350°.

Cut the slices of buttered bread into 4 pieces each. Place half in the bottom of a casserole; sprinkle with half the raisins, cinnamon, and lemon rind. Repeat. Beat the eggs and blend with the sugar. Stir in the milk and pour over the bread. Bake in a water bath for 1 hour. Serve warm.

Serves 6. About 250 calories each.

Ricotta Pudding I

Budino di Ricotta I

½ pound ricotta cheese
3 tablespoons light cream
2 tablespoons freeze-dried
  coffee

¼ cup sugar
3 tablespoons chopped
  walnuts

Cream the cheese and combine it with the cream, coffee, and sugar. Blend thoroughly and stir in the walnuts. Serve cold in sherbet glasses.

Serves 4. About 150 calories each.

Ricotta Pudding II

Budino di Ricotta II

4 eggs
¾ pound ricotta
¼ cup powdered or extrafine
  sugar

grated rind of 1 lemon
½ teaspoon almond flavoring

Preheat oven to 375°.

Separate the eggs and beat the yolks and whites separately. Sieve and smooth the cheese and combine with the egg yolks, sugar, lemon rind, and flavoring. Fold in the whites and pour into a buttered mold. Bake for 45 minutes. Chill.

Serves 6. About 150 calories each.

Strawberry Pudding

Budino di Fragole

2 packages (10 ounces each)
  frozen strawberries
2 tablespoons cornstarch

2 tablespoons rum, brandy, or
  sherry
1 teaspoon lemon juice

Thaw the strawberries in a strainer, saving the juice. Combine the cornstarch with the liquor and lemon juice in a saucepan and add the liquid from the berries. Heat for 2 minutes. Remove from the heat, cool slightly, and stir in the berries. Chill and serve in sherbet glasses.

Serves 4. About 110 calories each.

Chocolate Mousse I

Spuma di Cioccolata I

2 envelopes (½ ounce each)
  low-calorie chocolate
  pudding mix
2 cups skim milk

3 ounces semisweet chocolate
1 tablespoon instant coffee
  (preferably espresso)

Add the pudding mix to ½ cup of the milk and heat to dissolve. Add the chocolate, coffee, and the remaining milk and heat gently, preferably in a double boiler, while stirring, until the chocolate is melted and the mixture thickens. Pour into *pôts de crème* or after-dinner coffee cups. Chill for several hours and serve with small spoons.

Serves 6. About 125 calories each.

Chocolate Mousse II

Spuma di Cioccolata II

3 ounces sweet chocolate
¼ cup strong coffee
1 tablespoon Cointreau,
   Curaçao, or brandy

3 eggs, separated

Melt the chocolate in the coffee in a double boiler and cook until slightly thickened. Remove from the heat and cool. Whip the egg whites until stiff. Beat the yolks lightly with a fork and stir them into the cooled chocolate mixture. Fold in the egg whites and pour into small dishes such as after-dinner coffee cups or *pôts de crème* Chill for a few hours. Serve with small spoons.

Serves 4. About 175 calories each.

Coffee Mousse

Spuma di Caffè

1 envelope unflavored gelatin
1 cup light cream
2 tablespoons instant coffee
1 teaspoon cocoa

6 teaspoons sugar
2 eggs, separated
1 teaspoon lemon juice or
   vanilla extract

Dissolve the gelatin in the cream, stir in the coffee and cocoa, heat, and stir until the gelatin and coffee are dissolved. Cool. Add the sugar, whip in the beaten egg yolks, and fold in the stiffly beaten whites; add the flavoring. Taste for sweetness. Serve in small glasses, after-dinner coffee cups, or *pôts de crème*. Chill.

Serves 4. About 155 calories each.

Cold Espresso Mousse

Spuma di Caffè Espresso Freddo

1½ envelopes unflavored
    gelatin
1½ cups very strong coffee,
    preferably espresso
4 chocolate wafers

4 egg whites
¼ teaspoon cream of tartar
¼ cup sugar
1 teaspoon vanilla

Soften the gelatin in the coffee and heat until the gelatin is dissolved. Chill until thickened. Crush the cookies in a blender or food mill and stir the crumbs into the coffee. Beat the egg whites and cream of tartar until stiff. Beat in the sugar and vanilla and fold into the coffee mixture. Spoon into dessert dishes and chill for several hours.

Serves 6. About 80 calories each.

Coffee Whip

Sufflè di Caffè

2 envelopes unflavored gelatin
2 cups very strong coffee,
    preferably espresso

3 tablespoons sugar
4 egg whites
a pinch salt

Be sure to have very strong coffee.

Soften the gelatin in a cup of the cold coffee; heat with the sugar only until gelatin is dissolved. Chill.

Add the remaining coffee. Whip the egg whites with the salt until stiff. Fold into the cold coffee mixture. Taste for sweetness and chill again.

Serves 4. About 55 calories each.

Coffee Jelly

Gelatina al Caffè

2 cloves
1 stick or ½ teaspoon
  powdered cinnamon
¼ cup plus 1 tablespoon sugar

6 cups strong coffee
2 envelopes unflavored gelatin
1 cup skim milk, whipped
grated orange peel (optional)

Add the cloves, cinnamon, and ¼ cup of the sugar to 1½ cups of the coffee, cover, and heat for 5 minutes. Soften the gelatin in the remaining cold coffee, add to the hot, and stir until the gelatin is dissolved. Chill.

When firm, break into pieces with a fork and pile into sherbet glasses or a glass serving bowl. Top with or pass the whipped milk. (Skim milk will whip if you chill it very thoroughly, almost to the mushy stage. Add the remaining tablespoon of sugar when whipping.) Top with the orange peel, if you wish.

Serves 6. About 55 calories each.

Apple Meringue Soufflé

Sufflè di Mele

6 large apples
⅓ cup water
½ teaspoon cinnamon

4 egg whites
⅓ cup sugar

Preheat oven to 350°.

Peel, core, and dice the apples. Put in a pan with the water and cinnamon. Simmer until soft enough to mash easily. Remove from the heat.

Meanwhile, beat the egg whites until soft peaks form. Beat in the sugar, 1 tablespoon at a time, reserving 1 tablespoon.

Fold the mashed apples into the meringue. Put into a greased baking dish or 6 individual dishes. Sprinkle a little sugar on top and bake for 15 to 20 minutes. Serve at once.

Serves 6. About 150 calories each.

Orange Whip I

Spuma di Aranci I

1 envelope unflavored gelatin
1½ cups water
⅓ cup sugar

1 can (6 ounces) frozen orange
  juice concentrate
2 egg whites

Soften the gelatin in ½ cup of the water. Heat the remaining water and pour over; stir until the gelatin is dissolved. Add the sugar and orange juice concentrate and stir until the sugar is melted. Chill until slightly thickened; add the egg whites and beat with a rotary beater until fluffy. Put into a mold or serving bowl or individual molds or dishes. Chill.
  Serves 6. About 95 calories each.

Orange Whip II

Spuma di Aranci II

2 envelopes low-calorie orange
  gelatin
2 cups boiling water
1 cup orange juice

1 teaspoon lemon juice
grated rind of 1 orange
2 to 4 tablespoons sugar

Mix the gelatin with the boiling water and stir until dissolved. Add the remaining ingredients and taste for sweetness. Cool until thickened and whip. Chill, if you wish, or serve at room temperature in a bowl or individual dishes.
  Serves 8. About 55 calories each.

Strawberry Mold with Whipped Cream

Gelatina di Fragole con Panna Montata

2 envelopes low-calorie
  strawberry gelatin
2 tablespoons sugar
1 cup sliced strawberries

¼ cup heavy cream
1 teaspoon brandy, Triple Sec,
  or any fruit liqueur

Prepare the gelatin according to the package instructions. Put 1 tablespoon of the sugar on the berries and stir them into the gelatin. Pour into a bowl or mold and chill until firm.

Whip the cream, adding the remaining sugar 1 teaspoon at a time. Add the liqueur. Unmold the gelatin and top with the cream.

Serves 4. About 115 calories each.

Grape Whip

Gelatina d'Uva

1 cup boiling water	1 cup grape juice
1 envelope low-calorie orange gelatin	

Pour the water over the gelatin and stir until dissolved. Add the grape juice. Chill until thickened. Beat with a rotary beater until fluffy. Chill again until firm.

Serves 4. About 50 calories each.

Variations

Apple Whip

Gelatina di Mele

Use apple gelatin and apple juice in place of the orange and grape and follow the directions for Grape Whip*.

Pineapple Whip

Gelatina di Ananasso

Use pineapple gelatin and pineapple juice in place of the orange and grape and follow the directions for Grape Whip*.

MACAROONS

Macaroons, *amaretti,* are delicious cookie concoctions with an almond flavor. Invented in Italy, they are famous all over the world. Not too high in calories *by the piece,* they are hard to resist. It would be a great pity not to indulge in two or three, but don't be greedy!

Almond Macaroons I

Amaretti I

½ cup shelled almonds
⅛ cup bitter almonds

1 cup superfine sugar
2 egg whites

Preheat oven to 350°.

Grind the almonds together. Work in the sugar and egg whites until they form a paste. Make balls the size of a large marble or drop from a spoon in mounds the size of an olive onto a sheet of rice paper about 2 inches apart. You can do this on buttered brown paper or a greased cookie sheet instead of rice paper. Bake for about 20 minutes, until light brown. Cool before removing from the sheet.

About 30 macaroons. About 60 calories each.

Almond Macaroons II

Amaretti II

Since bitter almonds are not always available, this makes a good substitute.

1 can (8 ounces) almond paste
1 cup sugar

4 egg whites
2 teaspoons almond extract
pinch salt

Preheat oven to 350°.

Mix the almond paste and sugar together until smooth.

Add 2 of the egg whites and beat until very smooth. Beat the other 2 egg whites and a pinch of salt until stiff. Fold into the almond mixture. Add the almond extract. Drop by half-teaspoonfuls onto a greased cookie sheet about 2 inches apart. Bake for about 20 minutes, until lightly browned. Cool before removing from the sheet.

About 50 macaroons. About 55 calories each.

Almond Macaroons III

Amaretti III

½ pound shelled almonds
2 cups sugar

¼ teaspoon almond extract
2 egg whites, beaten

Preheat oven to 325°.

Grind the almonds until fine and mix with the sugar and almond extract. When thoroughly blended, fold in the egg whites. Make balls the size of a large marble or drop by half-teaspoonfuls onto a greased cookie sheet. Bake for about 10 minutes, until golden.

About 60 macaroons. About 50 calories each.

ICES

Italian ices are famous the world over. They are not a recent invention; they probably came to Italy from China centuries ago. In 1660 a Sicilian, Procopio, served ices in a restaurant. They consisted of frozen fruit juices, sometimes with water added. Some ices are still made that way: *granita di limone, granita di aranci.* Next came *sorbet,* sherbet, made with milk, and finally, ice cream, *gelato.* The skillful blending of fruit and other ingredients is a tribute to the fine Italian hand.

Fortunately, these ices may all be made in the freezer compartment of a refrigerator, which is much easier than the old-fashioned ice-cream-freezer method, and much, *much* easier than the original one, which consisted of digging a hole in the ground, filling it with snow and ice, and covering it with straw and wood. A frozen dessert is a fine ending for a meal — a light, tasty one after a heavy meal, and a richer ice cream for the climax of a light luncheon, dinner, or supper.

Water ices are beautifully low in calories, and sherbets, made with beaten egg whites or skim milk, are very little higher. These Italian ices will "make the end most sweet."

Coffee Ice

Granita di Caffè

¾ cup sugar   topping (optional)
½ cup water
3 cups very strong coffee
   (preferably espresso)

Put the sugar and water in a saucepan and simmer for several minutes until slightly thickened. Cool, add the cold coffee, stir, and pour into a bowl or refrigerator tray. Freeze only until mushy. Spoon into 6 thoroughly chilled parfait glasses. You may top with whipped skim milk (see page 267) or artificial dairy whip.

Serves 6. About 100 calories each without topping.

Variations

Orange Ice

Granita di Aranci I

Use 3½ cups orange juice instead of the coffee and ½ cup sugar instead of ¾ cup. Add 1 tablespoon lemon juice and the grated rind of 1 orange. Proceed as for Coffee Ice*.

Serves 6. About 120 calories each.

Very Orange Ice
Granita di Aranci II

1 can water
2 cans (6 ounces each) frozen
orange juice concentrate

2 tablespoons lemon juice
½ cup sugar

Add the water to the orange juice concentrate and stir in the lemon juice and sugar. Freeze for 1 hour, or until frozen around the edges and mushy in the middle. Remove to a cold bowl and beat with a rotary beater until smooth. Work fast. Refreeze for at least 1 hour.
Serves 4. About 160 calories each.

Lemon Ice
Granita di Limone

3 cups water
⅔ cup sugar

1½ cups lemon juice

Make a syrup with the water and sugar, cool, add the lemon juice, and freeze like Coffee Ice*.
Serves 6. About 110 calories each.

Melon Ice
Granita di Melone

1 ripe cantaloupe, about 1
pound
1 small honeydew melon,
about 1 pound

2 tablespoons lemon juice
¼ cup sugar

Remove all the flesh from the melons and purée in a blender or food processor with the lemon juice and sugar. Freeze immediately in a bowl or refrigerator tray until frozen around the edges and mushy in the middle. Remove and beat with a rotary beater and return to the freezer until frozen, about 2 hours.

Serves 4. About 115 calories each.

Wine Sherbet

Sorbetto di Vino

1 envelope unflavored gelatin
½ cup sugar
2 cups orange juice

1 cup dry wine: red, rose, or white
2 egg whites, beaten

Combine the gelatin and sugar with the orange juice and heat to dissolve. Add the wine and adjust sweetness to taste. Place into freezer trays or a bowl and freeze until mushy. Remove to a chilled bowl and beat until fluffy. Fold in the stiffly beaten egg whites. Refreeze until firm.

Serves 6. About 200 calories each.

Raspberry Sherbet

Sorbetto di Lamponi

3 packages (10-ounces each)
    frozen raspberries
1 teaspoon lemon juice

3 egg whites
2 tablespoons sugar

Thaw the raspberries and purée in a blender with the lemon juice; strain, forcing juice through a strainer with a spoon. Whip the egg whites until stiff. Beat in the sugar a tablespoon at a time. When stiff peaks form, fold in the raspberry purée. Place in the freezer compartment, set at its coldest point. This sherbet does not have to be beaten as it freezes.

Serves 6. About 150 calories each.

Peach Milk Sherbet
Sorbetto di Pesche

1 envelope gelatin	2 cups puréed peaches
½ cup sugar	2 teaspoons lemon juice
2 cups skim milk	2 egg whites, beaten stiff

Combine the gelatin and sugar with the milk and heat and stir until dissolved. Cool and add the peaches and lemon juice. Pour into a bowl or refrigerator trays and freeze until mushy. Remove to a cool bowl and beat until fluffy. Fold in the beaten egg whites and refreeze.

Serves 6. About 125 calories each.

Coffee Sherbet with Cream
Sorbetto di Caffè

4 cups boiling coffee	¼ cup cream, whipped
½ cup sugar	

Combine the coffee and sugar, put into a freezer tray, and, when mushy, beat with a whisk. Add the cream and refreeze. Serve in chilled glasses.

Serves 6. About 100 calories each.

Fruit Sherbet
Sorbetto di Frutta

1 envelope gelatin	1 tablespoon lemon or lime
½ cup sugar	juice
4 cups fruit juice: orange, pineapple, grape, or berry	2 egg whites, beaten stiff

Combine the gelatin and sugar in a pot, add the fruit juice, and heat to dissolve. Taste for sweetness. Freeze until the edges are firm and the center mushy. Remove to a cold bowl and beat thoroughly, then quickly fold in the beaten egg whites and refreeze.

Serves 8. About 100 calories each.

Vanilla Ice Cream

Gelato di Vaniglia

1 tablespoon cornstarch	3 teaspoons vanilla
2 cups skim milk	6 tablespoons sugar
½ cup evaporated milk	2 egg whites
1 envelope gelatin	¼ teaspoon cream of tartar
2 tablespoons water	

Make the cornstarch into a paste with a little of the milk. Add the remaining milk and evaporated milk, bring to a boil, and simmer for 3 or 4 minutes, until thickened.

Meanwhile, soften the gelatin in the water. Add to the milk and stir to dissolve. Add the vanilla and sugar and chill.

Beat the egg whites with the cream of tartar. Fold into the chilled mixture and freeze with the freezer turned to its coldest setting. You should not have to beat this, but if it seems icy as it freezes around the edges, remove to a cold bowl, beat, and refreeze.

Serves 6. About 115 calories each.

Variations

Peach Ice Cream

Gelato di Pesche

Fruit ice creams are made the same way. Use 1 cup less milk and reduce the vanilla to 1 teaspoon. At the last, add 1½ cups of mashed fresh peaches.

Serves 6. About 130 calories each.

Strawberry Ice Cream
Gelato di Fragole

Proceed as for Peach Ice Cream* but replace the peaches with 1½ cups of mashed fresh strawberries.
Serves 6. About 130 calories each.

Coffee Ice Cream
Gelato di Caffè

Add 2 tablespoons instant coffee, preferably Italian, to the Vanilla Ice Cream* mixture. Reduce the vanilla to 1 teaspoon.
Serves 6. About 115 calories each.

Index

Index 287